RECOPS

RecOps

**Recruiting Is (Still) Broken.
Here's How To Fix It.**

James Colino

LIONCREST
PUBLISHING

RECOPS

Recruiting Is (Still) Broken. Here's How to Fix It.

ISBN   978-1-5445-2669-0 *Hardcover*

           978-1-5445-2667-6 *Paperback*

           978-1-5445-2668-3 *Ebook*

To my Mom and Dad,

who taught me that anything can be fixed.

Contents

Introduction

I once took my recruiting team on a journey through a dangerous obstacle course...blindfolded. To ensure that we stayed connected, I lined everyone up single-file and joined them together at the waist with a rope. When all the knots were secured, I walked to the front of the line, tied the rope around my waist, and started walking forward. But I didn't tell them where we were going or what we were doing.

The location of the obstacle course was a local park. We were gathered in a flat, open field, standing in knee-high grass on the edge of a thick forest. Without warning, I started jogging at a slow pace across the field, heading toward the tree line. One by one, everyone stumbled forward as their section of the rope snapped tight and jerked them into motion. At first, it was fun. There was excitement, intrigue, and lots of laughter. As we got closer to the trees, however, I picked up the pace, and the excitement turned to anxiety because, remember, they were blindfolded, but I wasn't.

As we entered the forest, the team went silent. All I could hear was the sound of crunching leaves and twigs snapping beneath their feet as they tried to navigate the terrain in total darkness. Some of them tripped over logs. Some slammed into trees. I could tell by the amount of tension in the rope that they were struggling to keep up, but I continued to power through the course, dragging them with me at all costs.

As the journey intensified, team members started to show their true colors. Some of them emerged as leaders, shouting out instructions as they encountered obstacles. Others simply complained and wanted to stop. As I continued to sprint forward, weaving in and out of trees, I noticed that the tension in the rope gradually went slack, and their voices went silent once again. I thought to myself, *Yes! We're finally in sync!* But the opposite was true. When I stopped and turned around, I saw my team leaning against trees and sitting on logs, trying to catch their breath. They had removed the rope, taken their blindfolds off, and called it quits.

Before you report me to the local authorities for abusing my employees, I have to tell you that this story is not entirely real. But there is some metaphorical truth to it. This story is about me. Early in my career, an executive coach told me this story when I was making a transition from an individual contributor to a people manager. It was also at a time when the war for talent was in full swing, and an explosion of technology and innovation was disrupting the talent acquisition landscape.

The actual time frame was March 2013, and my coach from the Center for Creative Leadership in San Diego had just finished reviewing my 360-degree feedback. What he saw was encouraging but at the same time concerning. The encouraging part was that my colleagues felt like I was innovative and forward-thinking. They said I was always pushing the envelope and looking for new ways to transform our talent acquisition function. But the concerning part was that I moved too fast and enacted change without communicating the purpose or destination to my team very well. I wanted to fix everything. And I wanted to fix it now! As a result, they felt blindfolded, unable to keep up and unwilling to follow me down a difficult, unknown path in the dark.

I was stunned. But with one vivid metaphor and some additional guidance, my coach made two points very clear to me that day. He said, "Don't ever lose your forward-leaning approach to talent acquisition, but...

Set the stage for transformation by creating a clear vision for your team.

Create a system that drives ongoing transformation at a pace that your team and the organization can handle.

From that moment forward, this feedback set me on a journey to create clarity and find a continuous improvement practice for talent acquisition that would help me fix many of the biggest recruiting challenges I was facing. That search would lead me straight into the arms of a practice called RecOps.

A FORWARD-LEANING APPROACH

If you're like most recruiting professionals, you probably want to make your talent acquisition function better. The problem is, recruiting is hard. It's complex. It's full of stakeholders who have needs, biases, and opinions. Over the years, managing a recruiting function has been getting progressively harder to do. With the onslaught of software solutions flooding the market and the emergence of verticals for compliance, sourcing, branding, candidate experience, diversity, and more—recruiting leaders are simply overwhelmed. If you're one of them, on most days, you're just trying to keep your head above water. You live meeting to meeting, project to project, request to request, just trying to stay afloat. Every once in a while, you pull off a random process-improvement project. But then it's back to more urgent matters like opening new jobs, sourcing more candidates, and conducting more interviews.

It just never stops.

As the days and weeks fly by, you eventually lift your head and realize you're falling behind. Your employment brand needs a refresh. Your career site isn't mobile optimized. Your applicant tracking system (ATS) is out of date. Your boss wants a campus recruiting program. Your stakeholders want better reports. And then—BOOM!—you're so far behind that your chief executive officer (CEO) calls for a company-wide "reinvent recruiting" initiative. If you're lucky, you get to keep your job and spearhead the project.

This cycle of random, isolated improvements and big one-time optimizations is very much like dieting. It doesn't work over the long term. Like dieting, if you don't put systems in place to support a healthier lifestyle, you'll gain all the weight back (and then some). Talent acquisition is no different. It works better when you have a continuous approach to optimization. Ideally, your approach is forward-leaning. A forward-leaning recruiting function is one that doesn't accept the status quo. It doesn't wait to adopt new technologies. It brings solutions to the business before the business asks for them. It makes ongoing improvements based on a multiyear plan, not on a spur-of-the-moment pain point. And most of all, it's deliberate and centered on a clear vision.

In the absence of a forward-leaning mindset and practice, a recruiting leader will fall behind, lose control of their function, and live in a constant state of treading water. This book will help you prevent that from happening or dig you out of that mess if you're already in it.

THE IMPACT OF A SUBOPTIMAL FUNCTION

When a recruiting function is not optimized, an entire ecosystem of people suffers.

Your recruiting team suffers when inefficient processes and technologies require them to work longer hours and trudge through administrative tasks. Your hiring managers suffer because they go weeks, or sometimes months, without the talent they need to achieve their business objectives. Candidates suffer through overly complex online applications, a disjointed interview experience, and a general lack of transparency throughout the hiring process. Sometimes their families suffer, too, when a breadwinner gets screened out of your process for all the wrong reasons. It doesn't just hurt their career. It's hurting their ability to provide for their family.

And let's not forget about you. You suffer too. Because, at the end of the day, you're the one who shoulders the stress and overwhelm that comes from trying to make a talent acquisition function work. It's your career and your reputation on the line every time you get up in the morning to face another day.

The thing that frustrates me the most is that as recruiting professionals, we all know which aspects of our function need to be transformed. It's not a mystery. No matter what the size of your company is or where you're located in the world, we all want the same outcomes. We want better candidates, acquired faster, at a reasonable cost. And we want to deliver a good candidate and hiring manager experience in the process. But doing so has gotten increasingly more complex over the years. To achieve this universal promised land, it's critical that we have a system to fix what is broken and drive transformation in a more deliberate way.

THE SEARCH FOR A PRACTICE

Since the executive coaching session I mentioned earlier in this chapter, I've been on a mission to find a practice that would help me set a clear vision for my recruiting team and help us achieve our most ambitious goals. On this path, I've talked to many talent acquisition leaders, practitioners, consultants, and vendors. The best ones are always on this mission too. What I've learned over the years, however, is everyone has a different approach. We, as recruiting professionals, have a variety of tactics, tools, processes, and programs that we use. Many of them are very useful. But as an industry, we lack a unified practice that rolls up all of these proven techniques into an operational model. If we had a practice that had some definition to it, maybe—just maybe— we could all solve some of recruiting's biggest challenges through a common language and a common set of tools.

To understand the value of having a standard way of transforming a business function (or fixing part of a function), you need look no further than how your peers do it in other departments. If you're in a manufacturing setting, your production leaders have a lean manufacturing practice like Six Sigma that helps to reduce defects and lower costs. Your software developers use DevOps to more efficiently build software. Your marketing leaders use growth hacking and brand-building frameworks to unlock growth. Entrepreneurs and product managers use the lean startup method to build products that customers want. Even your sales leaders, who typically don't like to be bound by any sort of process, leverage the emerging practice of sales enablement to increase deal sizes and speed up sales cycles.

These standardized practices have fixed some of the biggest challenges faced by these functions. Entire industries of consultants and conferences have sprouted up as a result. But while other departments have developed these capabilities, what do recruiting departments have? What standard practice do we use for improving our processes, programs, and technologies? How do we consistently lower costs, increase speed, improve quality, or deliver a better hiring experience?

The truth is, we don't have a standard practice. The recruiting industry doesn't have a common way of making continuous improvements that lead to transformation. The most hopeful candidate for serving this purpose is just now beginning to take shape. And it goes by the name of RecOps.

WHAT IS RECOPS?

RecOps is a continuous improvement practice for the recruiting industry. Its primary purpose is to drive transformation through a deliberate focus on improving the recruiting process and key recruiting metrics. The target areas would include metrics related to experience, speed, cost, quality, and satisfaction. To do this, RecOps practitioners use proven techniques to mine data, build and manage recruiting programs, streamline processes, implement technologies, and enhance service delivery to both candidates and hiring managers.

Depending on who you talk to, RecOps is just a shorter way of saying recruiting operations. But I'd like to make the distinction that recruiting operations is typically a function that is most closely associated with scheduling interviews, running background checks, and other administrative duties. To be clear, this book is not about administrative duties. This book represents the evolution of the administrative side of recruiting operations into a more modern practice focused on recruiting optimization and recruiting transformation. This emerging field is called RecOps.

As a further point of clarification, RecOps is a term that is often used interchangeably with the terms *Talent Ops* or *HR Ops*. This is the result of the ongoing specialization that is taking place inside of HR departments across the world. For what it's worth, I believe these disciplines are close relatives of each other. They both focus on optimizing a specific vertical of human resources. I focus on the topic of recruiting, so I will use the term RecOps as a means to isolate it as a recruiting practice.

Throughout the remainder of this book, I'll expand upon the definition of RecOps and provide you with the information you need to start building your own practice in-house. Part 1 will cover an "Introduction to RecOps." I'll introduce a simple model to explain the important relationship between strategy, operations, and recruiting. In Part 2, I'll discuss "The Foundations of RecOps." These are three capabilities that serve as the foundation of a modern RecOps practice. Part 3 discusses the type of person who is best positioned to embrace and execute the transformation of your recruiting function. I call this "The RecOps Practitioner." Following these three heavy sections pertaining to the practice of RecOps, in Part 4, I'll pull back for some perspective on strategy and share one of the most important things you need to do before you embark on your RecOps journey. This part is called "Setting the Stage for Transformation." And finally, Part 5 will introduce "Putting RecOps into Practice." This section will provide a five-step tactical recommendation for how you can begin to improve any part of your recruiting function immediately through the practice of RecOps. A conclusion will serve to draw all we learned together.

I'VE HAD ENOUGH, AND I HOPE YOU HAVE TOO

In the pages that follow, I'll define RecOps and share some practices and tools that I have personally used or observed that have helped me (and others like me) to establish clarity and optimize functions in a continuous manner. I don't claim to be the "Father of RecOps" or the person who invented it, but I *am* putting a stake in the ground by attempting to give it shape and improving upon the existing concept through writing this book.

But why me? And why now?

The truth is, I didn't write this book to elevate my personal brand in the recruiting industry. And I certainly didn't write it to make money. Niche books like this almost never make money! As of the writing of this book, I'm right where I want to be as the practicing head of talent acquisition for Sheetz Inc., one of the largest and fastest-growing family-owned convenience store chains in America, with over 600 locations and 20,000 employees. Prior to this role, I managed a Fortune 500 global RecOps function at The Hershey Company, I served as the founder and CEO of a recruiting technology startup, and I led the technology-enablement function for Cielo, a world-class recruitment process outsourcing (RPO) company.

Over the course of this diverse twenty-year journey in recruiting, together with over two years of focused research on the topic of RecOps, I've solidified my belief that the key to running a world-class recruiting function lies in a leader's ability to build a mechanism for transformation. In this book, I'll refer to this mechanism as *the practice of RecOps*.

My experience and research have given me so much conviction in RecOps as a practice that I believe this book will help any HR or recruiting leader make improvements to their function, no matter their size, industry, or geographic location. I believe it will especially help those who are new to recruiting leadership or anyone who is experiencing some of the challenges and overwhelm that I listed earlier in this introduction. If we're being honest with ourselves, I think that covers just about everyone, myself included.

While my hope is that this book will help leaders optimize

their individual functions, I secretly hope it will spark a conversation and mobilize our industry around a practice that has the power to make the recruiting industry better as a whole. Since there are already a number of very capable people and organizations focused on improving different parts of the recruiting process, I've established a free website where you can learn more about RecOps and engage with established communities who can help you transform any part of your recruiting function. The website will serve as an extension of this book to pull all of the disciplines together and unite them through the lens of RecOps. You can access the website here: https://recops.org.

But back to the original questions: why me...why now?

Well, I've been in the recruiting space for my entire career. I've struggled with many of the same problems that you're probably facing right now. I've solved many of them, but every single day new ones emerge—labor market shortages, major economic shifts, advancements in technology, and even global pandemics! To stay nimble and competitive, these dramatic swings have created a need to have a forward-leaning, always-on approach to transforming a recruiting function, no matter what's happening in the world. It's never been more important than right now, in the face of a massive digital and mobile transformation. That's the *business* reason why I wrote this book. But there is a *personal* reason too. I genuinely want to help other talent acquisition professionals improve how their recruiting function operates. If just one struggling leader benefits from this book and it makes life easier for their recruiters, their hiring managers, their candidates, or themselves, then in my mind, all of the effort that went into writing this book will have been worthwhile.

Finally, if I'm being totally honest, there's one more reason. And it's a big one. I'm sick and tired of hearing business leaders, recruiting technology vendors, and candidates say that "recruiting is broken." It bothers me. But they're right! Despite all the advancements in recruiting technology, all the amazing recruiting conferences, all the best practices published online, and several decades' worth of improvements to our craft—recruiting, at far too many companies, is still broken. So, instead of denying that it's broken or doing nothing to fix it, I decided to write this book. If you're tired of hearing the negativity, too, I hope you'll join me in learning more about RecOps and the potential that it has to fix your recruiting function and our industry once and for all.

PART 1

Introduction to RecOps

CHAPTER 1

The Aha Moment

The first time I heard the term RecOps, I was on a call with the chief people officer (CPO) of a fast-growing startup in New York City. She was gearing up to double the size of the company and wanted to make sure her managers were using structured interview guides with professionally written interview questions. Fortunately, the software company that I owned at the time, HireBar, did just that.

At the end of the sales call, the CPO said, "I really like this. I'm going to put you in touch with my RecOps manager to finalize the contract and kick off the implementation."

At this point I had spent roughly fifteen years in the recruiting industry and had never heard the term RecOps. Despite feeling really dumb, I had to ask, "RecOps manager? What is that?"

She answered, "Oh, that's our fixer. She's our continuous improvement expert who sits on the talent acquisition team. She manages our tech stack, handles reporting, optimizes processes, builds programs, and generally ensures that everything works and we're always staying ahead of the curve."

Huh, I thought. That was my role for the last several years at The Hershey Company. But my title was different. At Hershey, I was called a manager of talent acquisition, technology, brand, and analytics. Different title but same duties.

Over the course of the next two years as the CEO of Hire-Bar, I kept bumping into these RecOps professionals when I met with new and prospective clients. They were usually on every sales call and always involved with the implementation. Some of them had the term RecOps in their title, but most of them didn't. They were called recruiting innovation managers, center of excellence (COE) leads, talent operations analysts, recruiting operations managers, and sometimes, just plain talent acquisition managers. But as I got to know some of them, I realized they were all doing mostly the same thing. They were all being charged with actively optimizing and transforming their recruiting function. Here are some common duties they shared:

- Performing process-improvement projects
- Designing better experiences for candidates and managers

- Building and maintaining referral, ambassador, and diversity programs
- Implementing and managing software systems
- Developing reports and dashboards
- Uncovering training and development opportunities for the recruiting team
- Researching recruiting innovation practices

While this small list of duties seems random, collectively, these activities are critical to achieving operational excellence. For example, one of the things I have always noticed about companies that had a RecOps person in place was that they were significantly easier to work with as clients. They implemented the HireBar software faster, had fewer problems with adoption, and got more out of the tool than companies that didn't have a resource in charge of ongoing transformation.

This experience was an aha moment for me. All I could think about was the advice that I got years earlier from my executive coach, who urged me to create an environment of clarity and a system of transformation. And it motivated me to explore RecOps on a deeper level. Even though I had been doing the equivalent of RecOps for several years, I realized that I could be more deliberate in my approach. And I would say the same about most of the practitioners I met. Collectively, we were all building a practice of recruiting optimization, but the projects we took on were often random and disconnected from a clear strategy or any sort of prioritization model. We were essentially playing whack-a-mole on problems as they bubbled to the surface. We were "fixers." I figured there had to be a better way.

Fast forward several years. After studying and experimenting with the craft of RecOps, I found there were some core activities, behaviors, and traits of the RecOps practitioners I met. I've organized that wisdom into this book in a manner I believe can help any HR or recruiting leader transform their function in a major way.

CHAPTER 2

The RecOps Model

A recruiting function is a dynamic system. Jobs become vacant. Recruiting kicks off. Candidates are contacted. Applicants are assessed. People get jobs. At a high level, that's how just about every recruiting function works. To support this flow of work, however, a highly complex ecosystem of people, processes, programs, and technology is required to keep the system working efficiently. The purpose of RecOps is to optimize this system in a strategic manner. By improving each part, you can transform the entire function.

To make this easier to digest, it's helpful to visualize a recruiting function with fewer components, more like a simple workflow than a complex network of moving parts that combine to deliver a hire. To illustrate this system, Figure 1 shows a typical recruiting function organized into just five components: strategy, operations, recruiting, data, and RecOps.

The RecOps Model

STRATEGY	OPERATIONS	RECRUITING	DATA	RECOPS
Mission	Processes	Kickoff	Cost	Data Analysis
Vision	Programs	Sourcing	Quality	Technology Enablement
Strategy	Technology	Advertising	Speed	
Goals	Compliance	Screening	Volume	Experience Design
Priorities	Budget	Scheduling	Experience	
	Training	Interviewing	Feedback	Continuous Improvement
	Reporting	Offers	Surveys	
	Calendars	Onboarding	KPIs	

Enhancements feed back into the system driving continuous improvement & transformation.

Figure 1

So as not to assume that we're on the same page about what each component means, I'm going to spend some time in the remainder of this chapter providing an explanation of each one and how this model can help you leverage clarity and continuous transformation to improve all or part of your recruiting function.

COMPONENT ONE: STRATEGY

"If you don't know where you're going, any road will take you there." This phrase is a catchy hook from the song "Any Road" by George Harrison of the Beatles fame. In life, a lack of direction can cause a delay in finding your true purpose. This can be relatively harmless over time. But in business, not knowing where you're going can be costly or can even tank your company. A lack of direction causes confusion within your employee base and can allow competitors to surpass you.

When running a recruiting function, creating ultimate clarity is essential. It helps a leader prioritize work that aligns to a strategy and a vision for the future. But it's not just about having clear goals. It includes having a clear mission, vision, and strategy too. These components help to establish purpose and direction for your team, while the goals serve to establish a focus for the improvements you want to make. Combined, it's a recipe for transformation. In Chapter 15 of this book, I'll cover these five components as a means for setting the stage for a successful RecOps practice. To clarify, these are the elements that are bundled together in the Strategy pillar:

1. Mission
2. Vision
3. Strategy
4. Goals
5. Prioritization

When you have these five clarifying elements in place, you will know both where you're going *and* the road that will take you there.

COMPONENT TWO: OPERATIONS

In many companies, the discipline of recruiting operations has existed for years. You might see it called talent operations or even HR operations. Sometimes it sits in a shared service center. No matter what you call it or where it sits, the majority of these functions are defined by a set of administrative duties as characterized by some the following tasks:

- Processing drug and background checks
- Assisting new hires with onboarding
- Scheduling interviews
- Booking interview-related travel
- Tracking expenses

While these tasks are incredibly important to running a high-functioning recruiting process, they merely scratch the surface of all the activities that go on behind the scenes of a busy recruiting department. If we really want to define the full set of tasks and manage them more effectively, we need to expand the scope of what we consider to be operations. If we view it through an expanded lens, it would include things like:

- Process management
- Program management (referral, diversity, campus, etc.)
- Reporting and analytics
- Recruiting compliance (OFCCP, EEO, GDPR, immigration, etc.)
- Technology administration (software, laptops, iPads, etc.)
- Employment branding and recruitment marketing
- Budgeting and contracts
- Team training and development

When you include these additional activities in the scope of operations, you expand and clarify your awareness of the things that underpin your hiring process. How well you manage all these activities will determine the overall health and success of your function. The building and optimizing of these programs and activities is a central responsibility of a RecOps practice. But it's more about optimization than it is about administration.

Taking this expanded viewpoint into consideration within a RecOps practice, operations can be defined like this:

> **Recruiting Operations is the complete set of activities, policies, processes, and programs that supports and enables your recruiting process.**

Now that we've established what is meant by operations, I'll move on to define what recruiting means as it relates to the model.

COMPONENT THREE: RECRUITING

If you picked up this book, I would assume that you have an idea of what recruiting is, but I'll clarify what it means within the context of this model. At most companies, recruiting is a general term that refers to an entire recruiting function or the entire set of services that a recruiting function delivers. Some of those services would include many of the operational tasks I listed in the last section—things like interview scheduling, recruitment marketing, or managing an employee referral program. But in an organization that has a RecOps practice, the definition of recruiting is narrower. Within this model, we define it this way:

Recruiting is the set of core steps that takes place in the process of filling a job.

AT MOST ORGANIZATIONS, IN THEIR MOST COMPLEX FORM, THESE STEPS INCLUDE THE FOLLOWING:

- Requisition initiation
- Strategy or intake meeting
- Sourcing and advertising
- Applicant screening
- Presentation of shortlist
- Candidate interviews
- Hiring team debrief
- Offer and pre-boarding

In the RecOps model, recruiting is deliberately separated from operations. The reason for this is to reinforce that one enables the other. Better operations enable better recruiting. For example, no talent acquisition leader is going to win an award for how well they schedule an interview or configure their applicant tracking system. But these are the exact things that enable a great hiring experience for candidates and hiring managers. But how do you know which part of your hiring process is not providing a great experience? The answer is by analyzing the data produced by your recruiting process.

COMPONENT FOUR: DATA

During the core steps of the recruiting process outlined in the system, data is collected. That data can come in many forms. It could be analytical data, such as the cost per applicant that comes from an advertising channel. Or it could be anecdotal, like the perception from a hiring manager that your hiring process is too slow. Either way, it's data that tells a recruiting leader how their function is performing. It's the fuel that a RecOps practice needs to identify problems and ignite change. So, to describe data as it pertains to the RecOps model, we can define it like this:

Data is the feedback produced during the recruiting process that is used to monitor performance and identify opportunities for improvement.

In Chapter 5, I'll go deep on how a RecOps practitioner can enable better analytics that will help you establish a system of data collection. For now, it's only important to understand that data is an essential component in the RecOps model because it's what tells you what is not working and how to measure transformation.

COMPONENT FIVE: RECOPS

At its core, RecOps is a practice designed to help recruiting leaders transform their function in a continuous manner. That's the simple definition. But let's explore some of the things that recruiting leaders typically like to improve when driving transformation. Here are a few examples:

- Job offer acceptance rate
- Cost per applicant
- Interview-selection accuracy
- Career-site conversion rate
- Quality-of-hire metric
- Number of employee referrals
- Hiring manager satisfaction rate
- Percentage of diversity hires

This list could go on and on. And it should. Because just about every area of recruiting has room for improvement. But while the bulleted list provides us with ideas of things to optimize, it's equally important for the model to clarify *how* these optimizations will get done. How they get done is through the practice of RecOps. This component represents a collection of proven tools, tactics, and methodologies that a practitioner can pull from, like levers, depending on the situation at hand. As you'll learn later in the book, there are three key levers—data analysis, technology, and experience design—that make up the foundation of a RecOps practice. For now, however, it's just important to restate the definition of RecOps as it relates to the model:

RecOps is a continuous improvement practice that leverages a variety of tools and tactics to transform all or part of a recruiting function.

Despite RecOps having proven tools, tactics, and methods, it's important to understand there are no hard-and-fast rules for how you fix whatever is broken in your recruiting function. The practice of RecOps is flexible and allows you to use the best tool for the job. For example, one of the hottest transformational tools that I see a lot of consultants emphasizing today is the use of candidate and hiring manager "journey mapping." This is a great idea for figuring out where you might have friction in your hiring process. But it's not the only way. You could also do a "process mapping" exercise and get similar results. Or you could do "empathy mapping" if you want to understand what your candidate and hiring managers are thinking, doing, and feeling at different parts of your process. Creating a "service blueprint" is also an effective tool to map the relationships between people, processes, and technology. The point is, in RecOps, the practitioner is free to leverage whatever they deem to be the best tool for the job or, in some cases, whatever tool they're most comfortable with.

THE FOLLOWING ARE SOME PROVEN AND POWERFUL METHODS (AND SKILLS) TO HAVE IN YOUR RECOPS TOOLBOX:

- Design thinking
- Lean Six Sigma
- Growth hacking
- Software adoption process
- Project management (Agile, Waterfall, Kanban, etc.)
- Program development
- Data analysis
- Instructional design
- Strategic planning

It's not necessary to invent a new technique to do RecOps. You can stand on the shoulders of the continuous improvement giants who came before and make massive enhancements to your function. To help drive this message home, in Chapter 7 of this book, I'll share some specific examples of how design thinking, data analysis, and a software adoption process can be leveraged to create operational improvements that can spark transformation. Later in the book, I'll unpack the exact skills and abilities that you'll want to look for when hiring a RecOps practitioner for your team.

THE INFINITE LOOP

In the RecOps model, you may have noticed there are dotted lines that originate from the RecOps pillar. These lines appear as arrows that cycle improvement efforts back into the strategy, operations, and recruiting pillars. While this isn't a physical component of the RecOps model, it should not be ignored. These lines serve to illustrate that transformation should be continuous. Isolated process improvement projects should not stop when the project is completed. The improvements should be fed back into the system and remeasured in a continuous loop to ensure that a performance improvement has taken place. This is a how a RecOps practice ensures that a recruiting function leans forward and never stagnates. In Part 5 of this book, called "Putting RecOps into Practice," I'll share how you can use a deliberate communication strategy, a series of specific meetings, and a project tracking tool to transform your function by creating a continuous loop of enhancements.

REFLECTION

In this chapter, I introduced a model to illustrate a simple way to look at how RecOps can impact a recruiting function in a continuous manner. A crystal-clear *strategy* along with strong *operations* will drive a high-performing *recruiting* process. And by paying attention to the feedback or *data* produced by the recruiting phase, you will identify how your function is performing and what needs to be improved. The practice of RecOps is how you make those improvements.

In the next chapter, I'll explain the difference between making one-off improvements to your recruiting function and driving ongoing transformation through a deliberate practice of RecOps. The power is in the practice!

CHAPTER 3

RecOps Is a Practice

Over the course of my life—usually during periods of high stress—I've turned to meditation to help quiet my mind. But it's never worked for me! My mind always races out of control, and no matter what I do, I can't calm it down. On top of that, when I try modeling the sitting posture of those spiritual gurus I see online, my back hurts. It feels weird, and I just end up getting more frustrated. I must have tried meditation unsuccessfully about a thousand times! In the end, I concluded that meditation is simply not for me. Until I met Sam.

I had just boarded a flight from San Diego to Philadelphia. It was a five-hour, nonstop red-eye. This was the return leg of the flight that took me to the Center for Creative Leadership, where I met the executive coach who started me on my RecOps journey. As I forced my large bag into a tiny space in the overhead compartment, I turned and noticed a man sitting next to me in the window seat. He had his legs crossed and eyes closed. The back of his hands were resting on his knees, with his thumb and index finger touching in the "okay" position. He was in a deep meditative trance. I was jealous. He looked so relaxed, and I was wound tight and clammy, like I normally am at takeoff.

Shortly after we reached cruising altitude, this man, who I still only know as Sam, came out of his trance just in time for the beverage service. I don't normally talk to people on flights, but I was curious about why he was meditating. So, I struck up some small talk.

"So how long have you been meditating?"

Without turning his head to look at me, he said, "The day after my first flight."

As it turned out, Sam and I shared an extreme fear of flying. He explained to me that meditation had cured his fear. As we talked more, he also told me that it had transformed his life in many other ways too.

Intrigued but wanting to share my experience with him, I chimed in, "I've tried to meditate about a thousand times. But every time I try, I can't quiet my mind. I feel awkward.

I get frustrated, and I end up quitting or falling asleep. It doesn't work for me!"

He finally cracked a smile, but still looking straight ahead, he hit me with a simple but profound statement: "If you want to experience transformation, you must establish a *practice* of meditation."

The way he emphasized the word "practice" piqued my interest, so I inquired, "What exactly is a *practice* of meditation?"

"A practice is a routine. It's the ongoing pursuit of improving the routine." He went on to explain that there is no one way to practice meditation. But that doesn't mean that it lacks structure or time-tested rituals that have worked for centuries. "When you establish a routine of quieting your mind, you get better and better at it over time." (FYI, Sam had a funny way of speaking in rhymes during our conversation.)

Sam and I continued our discussion as the cabin lights dimmed and passengers went to sleep. Over the next hour, he shared with me eight things that I should think about when establishing my own practice of meditation. I wrote them all down on my beverage napkin:

EIGHT KEYS TO BUILDING A
MEDITATION PRACTICE

- **Goals:** define what you want to get out of your practice.
- **Time:** pick a specific time of day to practice.
- **Place:** establish a quiet and comfortable meditation space.
- **Posture:** sit in a comfortable position, palms up, with your thumb and index fingers touching.
- **Breathe:** learn how to belly breathe through your nose.
- **Routine:** meditate every day, even if it's only for five minutes.
- **Mantra:** introduce mantras to overcome mind-racing.
- **Community:** find a community to learn from and deepen your practice.

When the plane landed, we didn't exchange contact information, but I committed to Sam that I would define my routine and begin a practice of meditation immediately. And I did. That week and in the weeks that followed, I committed to practicing at the same time every day upon waking. As I did this, my sessions got longer. My moments of clear-headedness got easier. I could focus for longer periods of time. I got frustrated less, got more work done, and transformed my relationships with people who used to get under my skin. Not only had I improved all of those things, but I could now drop myself into a deep meditative state whenever I flew. This has been a game-changer for me. What was the difference-maker? I committed to building a structured practice. It was this insight, coupled with the feedback I had received from my executive coach just a day earlier, that led me down the path of developing a formal practice of RecOps.

WHY DEVELOP A PRACTICE?

Do you really have to create a practice of RecOps to transform some aspect of your recruiting function? The answer is no. You could certainly chip away at a process here or a program there and make incremental gains. It's what most companies do. But the questions you need to ask yourself are these: To what degree do you want to transform? How quickly? How dramatically? How much longer can you afford to wait before you improve your outdated technologies or disjointed experiences that cause more work for your team? How many more times do you want to hear someone say that "recruiting is broken"? For the most progressive recruiting leaders around the world, the answer is: enough is enough! It's time to fix recruiting, and the time to do it is now!

The power of having a deliberate practice specifically focused on transformation is that you can create community around the effort. You can establish best practices that can be adopted and standardized in ways that don't exist today. While I'm not suggesting that RecOps can have the same global impact that lean manufacturing had on the automobile industry, I do think it has the potential to have a parallel effect. When Toyota introduced lean manufacturing to the world, it had a profound impact on the speed, quality, cost, and innovation of car production—so much so that other industries, from motorcycles to healthcare to recruiting, have borrowed the methods. Other systems of transformation like DevOps, growth hacking, sales operations, and the lean startup movement are all having a similar impact. The reason for this widespread transformation is that a committed group of practitioners took it upon themselves to develop and deploy a practice. I hope those of you who are reading this book can help do the same thing for the recruiting industry.

THE PRACTICE OF RECOPS

When I learned that meditation could be improved by defining a practice, it reminded me that just about everything in life and business can be transformed with a deliberate approach. And while RecOps is just in its infancy, it does have some defining characteristics that can be structured into a practice. I developed these through my work at Pfizer, Hershey, HireBar, Cielo and Sheetz. I also learned by observing practitioners who were transforming their recruiting functions all over the world. These characteristics, which are introduced below, serve as the backbone of this book. They help to differentiate a recruiting department that has a RecOps practice from one that is simply performing process improvements from time to time. The five defining characteristics will serve as a quick introduction to core elements of a RecOps practice, and the remaining sections of the book will provide a deeper explanation. Those sections are noted in the parenthesis.

THE HIGH-LEVEL COMPONENTS
OF A RECOPS PRACTICE:

A Model: the RecOps model is used as a framework to understand the relationship between strategy, operations, recruiting, data, RecOps and continuous improvement.

(Part 1: Introduction to RecOps)

Foundational Activities: core activities are centered on three levers: enabling insights, embracing technology, and designing experiences.

(Part 2: The Foundations of RecOps)

Dedicated Resources: a specific person is dedicated to and responsible for uncovering, owning, and driving the projects that will drive transformation.

(Part 3: The RecOps Practitioner)

Clarity: a mission, vision, and strategy have been developed, coupled with a system of prioritization, to drive focus and clarity.

(Part 4: Setting the Stage for Transformation)

Practice Management: a defined plan, tracking tools, and communities are leveraged to help operationalize RecOps and manage it as a practice.

(Part 5: Putting RecOps into Practice)

Over the remainder of this book, we'll unpack each of these areas in more detail so that you can begin to build your practice and deliberately transform your function without delay.

PART 2

Foundations of RecOps

CHAPTER 4

Foundational Activities

Never in the history of our profession has recruiting been so complicated. To run a recruiting function today, the sheer number of moving parts you need to manage is mind-boggling. Not to mention all the trends and advancements in technology you need to keep up with just to stay current in your field. To survive today, let alone thrive, a recruiting department must master some core activities that enable the ongoing transformation of the function. I call these core activities the foundations of RecOps.

Up until this point, I've mostly focused on the theory of RecOps. I introduced a model to help explain some key components that enable a mindset of continuous transformation. I also covered five high-level components that, when put into place, define a RecOps practice. But I haven't gone deeper to provide examples of the type of work that can be performed by a RecOps practitioner. I haven't explained how to "do" RecOps. In this section, I'll begin that discussion with a focus on three activities that sit at the heart of a forward-leaning practice. These foundational activities give you the modern tools to fix recruiting even during the most difficult situations. At a high level, they help a recruiting function deal with the challenges of the data-rich, tech-heavy environment we work in today. These activities include:

- Enabling insights
- Embracing technology
- Designing experiences

These three activities are core fundamentals in a practice of RecOps because they are the modern tools of transformation. They allow a recruiting leader to uncover problems, automate processes, and create consumer-grade experiences that fix many disjointed components of recruiting today.

In the remainder of this section, I'll provide examples of how to better enable insights; how to select, implement, and adopt technology; and finally, how to leverage both data and technology to create amazing experiences for your candidates and internal stakeholders. As an advanced warning, this chapter will get a little bit technical and tactical. While this isn't a "How to Do RecOps for a RecOps Practitioner" book per se, my hope is that it sets the tone for the types of activities that a RecOps practitioner would do on their path to optimizing a recruiting function. At the same time, it provides insights into some specific tactics that have proven to be successful at transforming recruiting activities at large global companies that have a RecOps practice in place. Let's begin by reviewing a case study of how to set up the capability to leverage data in a big way.

CHAPTER 5

Enabling Insights

One of the best ways to liberate yourself from the stress and overwhelm that comes from running a talent acquisition function is to get your data under control. Building strong analytical capabilities is also the smartest way to diagnose problems in your function and fix them using a data-driven approach. That's why data is one of the key components in the RecOps model.

To be clear, though, I'm not talking about cobbling together your weekly applicant tracking system report in Microsoft Excel. I'm talking about grabbing your data by the scruff of the neck and forcing it to reveal all the magical insights that lie hidden in your systems.

Several years ago, this used to be hard. In some cases, it was impossible. But we live in a world today with experts who know how to automate the extraction of data from your systems, properly format it, and use visualization tools to bring it to life. And yet the vast majority of recruiting organizations are still struggling to create and distribute even the most basic reports to their business leaders, let alone glean insights from the data. It's time to move on from that approach. We can do so much better.

Getting your data under control does a number of things for you. It—

- Gives you the confidence to make more informed, data-driven decisions
- Provides credible answers to difficult questions from executives
- Quantifies the value that your team delivers to the organization
- Uncovers the truth about your function, good or bad
- And, most importantly, *enables the insights* that you need to transform your function

The *Harvard Business Review* defines *insights* as "actionable, data-driven findings that create business value." The key terms here are "actionable" and "business value." The power is not in the data itself. It's what you do with the insights that matters.

In this chapter, my goal is to help you think bigger about how to manage your data and enable more advanced capabilities. These techniques should live at the heart of your RecOps practice. As a heads-up, this section will be more technical than previous chapters. My intent is not to overwhelm you but to provide you with some context that will start you down a path of doing your own discovery. This isn't a "how to" manual that you can put in place overnight either. It will most likely require assistance from information technology (IT) or human resources information technology (HRIT). But if you're committed, you can bake these ideas into the foundation of your RecOps practice and *enable insights* in new and valuable ways. Let's start with the most basic of questions: "What do you want to know about your recruiting function?"

ASKING GOOD BUSINESS QUESTIONS

Asking good business questions is the first step in enabling insights. Rather than copying your metrics from a recruiting industry best practices white paper, start by asking yourself, "What are the questions I'm trying to answer about my function?" When you approach it this way, you will end up with analytics that help you solve your unique business problems rather than generating pretty dashboards that simply display historical data.

To make the process of deciding what to measure easier, it's helpful to segment your insights into two categories: operational and diagnostic. You can think of operational data as the analytics that you want to measure on a regular basis. It usually makes up the core metrics that provide insights about the health of your function.

Here are some sample "operational" questions you might want to monitor year-round:

- Which of our recruiting channels are most effective?
- What is our average time to hire by department and location?
- What percentage of candidates decline our jobs?
- How many jobs did we open, close, and cancel over a specific period of time?

Diagnostic data refers to the pursuit of an answer to a specific question or the desire to find the root cause of a recruiting problem. Below are several examples of diagnostic questions that can help you improve your function. As you'll note, this type of data rarely shows up on dashboards. It usually ends up in a custom graphic that tells a story about a complex recruiting challenge. Some sample questions are:

- Why did we come up short on filling our sales recruiting class last month?
- Do we have enough recruiters to fill the openings we have forecasted for next quarter?

- Is there a correlation between LinkedIn Recruiter logins and sourcer submittal rates?
- Does our marketing team select diverse candidates at the same rate as other departments?

If you consider your analytics practice essential to delivering two types of insights, you will begin to build two different muscles. One muscle is automating data extraction for your core *operational* data. The other is structuring your data sets in such a way that you can easily diagnose a specific situation. Your RecOps practice should help you do both. In the next section, I'll go a little deeper into how you can make this possible.

Before we go there, however, I want to make a point about the role that your technology vendors play in helping you to enable insights. They can make it really easy for you or darn near impossible. So, when choosing a technology partner (ATS, CRM, TRM, etc.), be sure to do a thorough review of their analytics capabilities.

As a baseline, look for solutions that allow easy access to your full set of data. Also, look for solutions that provide built-in insights that were never possible before. For example, a technology startup named Goodtime in the interview logistics space is enabling new insights that companies couldn't get before. Goodtime helps recruiting coordinators schedule interviews faster by automating tasks that are normally manual. For instance, searching for calendar availability and matching interviewers to a panel. Goodtime's architecture and reporting engine allows them to capture answers to questions that were never possible before, such as:

- How often is a certain manager interviewing each week?
- Who among my managers has been certified to interview?
- Do we have enough trained interviewers to meet our upcoming interview volume?
- Who are my best interviewers? Who are my worst?
- Who cancels interviews most frequently or at the last minute?

Answers to questions like these can turbocharge your assessment capabilities, help you hire better people, and provide a better candidate experience. But it would be really hard to measure these things if you're still manually scheduling your interviews. Taking risks on new technologies can be a great strategy to enable unique and powerful insights. Thinking about how you manage your data *as a practice* is imperative.

THE CIELO APPROACH TO INSIGHTS

Adam Godson, the former recruiting technology leader for Cielo Talent, took recruiting data to a whole new level. If you're not familiar, Cielo is an RPO. RPO stands for recruitment process outsourcing. Businesses in this category provide plug-and-play recruiting services for all or part of a recruiting function. Cielo is routinely rated as one of the top RPOs in the world by the organizations that measure such things. I had the pleasure of working at Cielo, where I saw firsthand how world-class talent acquisition can be delivered across any industry anywhere in the world.

As an organization, Cielo serves over one hundred clients of all sizes globally. As a part of their solution, they're responsible for enabling insights for their clients across a wide variety of technology systems. As Cielo's customer base grew, they found themselves building out a small army of reporting analysts. Each one was assigned to handle reporting needs for a given set of clients. Each week they raced to extract data, build spreadsheets, and update dashboards. The dashboards were great, but they were static. Invariably, an HR leader or business executive from a client would ask a question that couldn't be answered by the outdated and predefined dashboards.

According to Adam, these questions occurred quite frequently, and they threw the reporting analysts into a minor tailspin because they had to extract the data (again), massage it into a certain format over the course of a couple of days, consult with their Cielo account leaders, and then create a visualization that illustrated an answer to the original question. Usually, the answer came several days later and at the cost of disrupting the workflows (and stress levels) of both analysts and Cielo account leaders.

To fix this situation in a strategic way, Adam looked at data management as a practice and started with a simple business question: "How might we use technology to give our clients the power to search their own data whenever they want to?" This seemed like a reasonable but extremely complex request when you consider that he had over one hundred clients who were using twenty-seven different applicant tracking systems, all configured differently!

While you might only be dealing with data from a single applicant tracking system, bear with me because the process to extract, organize, and analyze your data is essentially the same.

Adam's goal with this initiative, as we defined in the last section, was to answer business questions and deliver two capabilities: operational and diagnostic insights. To do this, he needed a way to extract data from key recruiting systems, clean it up, and push it into a single interface that could be used to visualize the data for gathering insights.

Even though Adam and his team are highly technical and represent exactly the type of professionals you need to power a RecOps practice, he sought the help of a consultant to develop a strategy and execute the vision. This is an important point. As you build your RecOps practice, don't let a lack of technical knowledge prevent you from improving some aspect of your function. There are experts who can educate and guide you on your journey, solving problems as they arise. At most organizations, you might actually have someone in-house with this expertise. So, as you consider building out your analytics practice, look to your internal IT or HRIT resources first. They might have the software tools and the expertise to make this easier (and less costly) than you might think. Just be sure not to get lost in a long queue of IT projects that may have a higher priority!

In Cielo's case, the size and scale warranted the hiring of two data scientists who had expertise with a cloud-based data visualization tool called Birst. Led by Kevin Nass, Cielo's Senior Manager of Technology Solutions, they started working with each Cielo client one by one in two-week sprints. Rather than trying to work with all of their recruiting platforms, they kept it simple by working first with applicant tracking system data. But the long-term goal was to pull in data from multiple systems in an effort to connect advertising, interviewing, feedback, and sourcing data into a single source of truth. To further clarify how you can do this, I'm going to go a little deeper on the process.

To begin, let's look at a visual of how to get data from multiple systems into a format that will allow you to create meaningful dashboards and diagnose complex issues. As you'll immediately notice in Figure 2, this process is probably much more complex than the manner in which you obtain reports today. You probably get that information by clicking a "download" icon in your ATS. It might even be automatically sent to your inbox. But then you have to manipulate the data using Excel or Google Sheets. The resulting dashboards are out of date by the time you email them to all your stakeholders.

If this sounds familiar or if you've ever been frustrated by the reporting capabilities of your systems, you can follow in Cielo's footsteps and transform your analytics capabilities. Think of the process as having three stages: extract, organize, and visualize. Let's review each step at a high level.

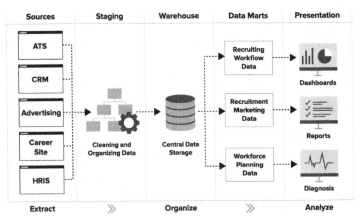

Figure 2

STEP 1: EXTRACT

To begin the process of enabling insights, the first step is mapping the fields in the systems that you'll be extracting data from. Your systems are called sources. By identifying and labeling all the fields that are available to extract, you'll be able to organize the data much easier for analysis. It's important to have a clear and common language for your fields. This allows you to connect data points from multiple systems into a single dashboard or visual.

Once the data mapping exercise is complete, you can begin to extract data in the format you designed. This involves pulling the information out of your systems. Depending on the sophistication of your source, you might need to work with your vendor to obtain a flat file (like a .csv document) or gain access to an API. API is an acronym that stands for application programming interface. An API is simply a software tool that allows two applications to talk to each other. This is typically the preferred method for extraction because it allows for an automated, direct feed of data from your ATS (for example) to your central data warehouse or visualization tool. For many recruiting systems, there are integration tools, such as Dell Boomi, Jitterbit, or Cloud Connectors, that have prebuilt connections to the API, so pulling data out can be made even easier. Automating the extraction process should be one of your key objectives because this will save you a tremendous amount of time and keep your data fresh.

If your technology vendor does not have an API, flat file extraction can still be automated. But this process involves using a third-party tool so you don't have to do a manual extraction every time you want to look at your data.

STEP 2: ORGANIZE

Once you have identified the data you want to pull and have a means for automating the extraction, you'll want to push that data into what is called a staging area. Staging is an important step where your raw data is cleaned up and organized according to a set of rules that you define. This step allows you to structure your data so that you can "pull" reports and create visualizations that actually make sense to an end user.

The data then moves from staging to the data warehouse. The warehouse is a central storage area where all the data sits, ready to provide you with insights. Depending on how much and what kind of information you're storing, the data in your warehouse can be further organized into what are called data marts. You may also hear them be called cubes. These are simply categories of data that are commonly grouped together. Some examples of data marts in talent acquisition would be your workflow, recruitment marketing, or workforce planning data.

STEP 3: ANALYZE

The final step in the process is creating a mechanism for accessing your data for diagnostic or visualization purposes.

This typically involves a tool such as Birst, Tableau, PowerBI, Google Data Studio, or something similar. These tools provide you with the capability to diagnose one-off issues and make beautiful, automated, cloud-based dashboards that your stakeholders can view online. This means you can eliminate your weekly dashboard scramble in Excel and provide more modern, powerful analytics to your business. That's what Cielo did, at scale.

It took Adam and his team nearly eighteen months to get the ATS data from over one hundred clients into their cloud platform called SkyAnalytics, but the results were amazing. Today, Cielo clients now have 24/7 access to their recruiting analytics in the cloud. The dashboards can be customized at the user level so only the data that is relevant to their needs is displayed. But if they want to go deeper to answer a more specific question, the data is organized and ready to explore.

Cielo is now processing and displaying over twenty million data points to its clients' users on a weekly basis. They also provide full access to historical data, current data, and even some predictive forecasting. And this data is no longer being handled manually by teams of Excel experts. This, of course, had some financial benefits for Cielo, but, more importantly, it delivered a powerful solution to their clients that was better and faster.

Adam's willingness to bring in outside expertise and his

refusal to accept the old way of reporting has won praise from his clients and consistently earned Cielo awards from the Everest Group and Nelson Hall, with both citing Cielo as the world's most technology-enabled RPO.

REFLECTION

In the RecOps model provided in Part 1 of this book, I mentioned that data plays a critical role in identifying the areas of your function that you need to optimize. To do this, it's critical that you take a more strategic approach to extracting, organizing, and analyzing the data from your systems. To make this happen, you may need to bring on an expert to help you. To harness your data in more beneficial ways, you'll also need to embrace technology in new and different ways. In the next section, let's look at how your RecOps practice can create a machine for finding, selecting, and implementing technologies that have the power to transform your function.

CHAPTER 6

Embracing Technology

Right now, there are technologies on the market that could transform your recruiting function.

You probably know that. But there are barriers to putting these tools in place, aren't there? Things like money, time, resources, and know-how.

The biggest barrier, though, is *fear*.

There are so many technology choices on the market today, and you don't know who to trust. You've also been burned before. You put your neck on the line and invested in a product that claimed to solve all of your problems, and it didn't work.

When we, as recruiting professionals, feel vulnerable due to a lack of trust or knowledge, we don't take risks. This fear leads to withdrawal. So, we don't engage with software vendors. We don't experiment with pilot programs, and we miss software solutions that could eliminate some of our biggest problems.

Fortunately, one of the benefits your RecOps practice can deliver is to help you reduce those fears by understanding the technology market and providing a structured way to implement solutions. If you can do that successfully, you can lean into the future and become a case study for robotic process automation, artificial intelligence, machine learning, augmented reality, or whatever they produce next!

But how do you do that without recklessly piloting every tool on the market?

The answer, like other answers in this book, is by leveraging your RecOps practice to bring structure to your approach. While adding structure is not often correlated with being innovative, you don't want to add more chaos to your function by blindly adding new tools to your technology stack. You want your RecOps practitioner to help you experiment responsibly with the latest solutions. But you also need them to help you guarantee successful implementation and long-term adoption for the tools you select. In this chapter, I'll cover four ways you can embrace the future and ensure successful adoption. The following action steps will get you there:

- Create a technology roadmap.
- Establish a learning system.
- Use structured experimentation.
- Design adoption strategies.

Let's look at how you can leverage each of these strategies.

CREATE A TECHNOLOGY ROADMAP

To reduce the confusion and overwhelm associated with the crowded technology marketplace we have today, it's wise to narrow the scope of what you're looking at. You can do that by creating a technology roadmap.

A technology roadmap is simply a documented plan for what your technology stack looks like today and what it will look like a year, two years, and three years from now. If you don't have a roadmap, then you'll find yourself chasing the next shiny new toy and buying tools you don't need. You'll also hang on to tools you should get rid of, which wastes money and hurts productivity.

Doing a roadmap has numerous benefits. Here are just a few:

- It helps you budget for future investments.

- It allows you to collaborate early with key stakeholders in IT, HRIT, or purchasing.
- It allows you to forecast the people you need to implement a new tool.
- It keeps you focused on the future but grounded in reality.

A roadmap doesn't have to be complicated to be effective. You can create one using tools you already have, such as MS PowerPoint or Google Slides. Your roadmap should include the following components:

SLIDE 1: YOUR VISION FOR TECHNOLOGY

This is a narrative that describes the vision you have for your technology program. Will you be "the most technologically advanced recruiting function in the world, deploying best-of-breed solutions"? Or will you "seek to unify the recruiting technology stack through a single enterprise platform"? The vision slide is where you want to look out into the future and paint a picture of your ideal technology environment.

SLIDE 2: CURRENT TECHNOLOGY STACK

This slide should be a table listing your current technology investments, number of licenses, annual costs, and when the licenses expire. You should also include which technologies you plan to stabilize, expand, or sunset.

SLIDE 3: CURRENT YEAR INITIATIVES

On this slide, you'll get more granular with a simple table showing the projects you plan to pursue in the current calendar year. You'll want to identify the various categories of tech to help other stakeholders understand the complexity of your ecosystem. Include categories such as ATS, customer relationship management (CRM), recruitment advertising, onboarding, sourcing, scheduling, etc. You could even get more granular by adding some sample tasks you want to complete within each of your projects.

SLIDES 4 AND 5: YEAR TWO AND THREE INITIATIVES

These two slides are essentially the same as Slide 3, but they look out into the future at projects two and three years from now. You don't need to get too specific here with tasks, but you'll want to lay out your long-term strategy. This is where you can dream about pushing the limits and trying new things. You can always make adjustments over time.

If you scan the QR code in Figure 3 with a capable mobile device, you can view an example of a sample roadmap in Google Slides. You can also access all the free resources mentioned in this book. If you prefer to type in a web address, everything can also be found at https://recops.org/book/resources.

Figure 3

Having a visual representation of your current and future technology investments will help you identify where to focus your time in the coming months and years. It puts you in the driver's seat for identifying innovation in certain categories, as opposed to feeling like you need to understand the entire ecosystem.

The most important benefit to having a technology roadmap is that it ensures your technology stack is current. If you're going to build a forward-leaning recruiting organization, this is where you can make the biggest impact. One of the biggest complaints that candidates and hiring managers have about the hiring process is that our technologies are clunky and out of date. Hiring is broken in part because our technologies are broken, or at least, they haven't been properly implemented or integrated. Having a technology roadmap brings visibility to your gaps and helps you create action plans to create a more consumer-like experience across your recruiting services.

To keep your roadmap current, you need a strategy for keeping up with the latest tools on the market. As we discussed in

Part 1 of this book, there are hundreds or maybe thousands of tools out there. As a result, you need a plan for product discovery within the context of your roadmap. The best way to do this is by assigning your RecOps resource to establish a routine for finding relevant technologies and bringing them back to the team for consideration. You might also want to establish your own routine for staying informed.

ESTABLISH A LEARNING SYSTEM

I saw a bumper sticker a few years ago that read, "If you're not keeping up, you're falling behind." Duh, right? Well, this simple and obvious phrase stuck with me over the years, and I think it's quite relevant to the world of technology that we're living in today. To stay current with the rapid pace of innovation and identify the game-changing tools that you need to transform your function, you need a structured plan for keeping up with it. You can't sit back and assume that ideas and information will come to you serendipitously. Yes, you'll get plenty of calls and emails from technology vendors who will introduce you to their products and services, but you need a plan that operates on your terms.

If you've completed your technology roadmap as I described in the previous section, then you'll be more focused on the areas of technology you might want to try. From there, you or your RecOps lead can dive into the wide array of information that is available.

Following are four of my favorite ways to uncover the tools you'll need to supercharge your technology roadmap and take your function to the next level:

- **Podcasts.** Audio is one of the easiest ways to stay current on recruiting trends because the content is happening in near real time. It's also convenient because you can learn passively while you're driving, shopping, or taking a shower. Most podcast apps allow you to listen to the content at 1.5x or 2.0x speed too. I usually listen at 2x because I'm pressed for time, and it allows me to cover more ground. I also listen to a wide range of podcasts both inside and outside of the recruiting space.
- **Online Communities.** With a simple search on Google, Facebook, or LinkedIn, you can easily find groups to join. In addition to groups, there are also Slack channels and online communities that are both paid and free on topics like candidate experience, HR technology, recruitment marketing, and more. These groups are a great way to learn from your peers and get advice about how to solve some problems you might be experiencing. They represent places where you can get help, have conversations, lurk, and learn. Communities are so important that I'll cover them on a deeper level in the last part of this book.
- **Specialized Conferences.** Conferences are a great way to stay current on what's happening in your industry. I find that *general* conferences tend to be less valuable than specialized ones. For example, you'll learn more

about sourcing by going to SourceCon, and you'll get better insights about a software tool by attending that company's user conference. Almost every software vendor these days has their own user conference. Just go to their website and look for "events."

- If you can't afford to go to conferences, don't like to travel, or can't travel because of a global pandemic, many organizers have started to livestream the sessions online at a lower cost or even for free. You can watch them live or watch a recorded version on YouTube. I keep a running list of conferences here: https://recops.org/events. Review this list during your budgeting season and make sure to get a couple of relevant events on your annual calendar.

- **Coffee Talks.** As of the writing of this book, the COVID-19 pandemic has put a damper on human-to-human discussions, but prior to that, I found that coffee (and beer) is a great way to connect. I had many cups of coffee (and pints) with recruiting leaders and RecOps practitioners while writing this book. My strategy for inviting peers to join me is to invite people who are already putting themselves on display as open connectors. If you want to have coffee talks, pay attention to the practitioners who are speaking at conferences and people who are active on social media. They are more inclined to have one-on-one conversations with you. If you can't physically have coffee, the phone is still an amazing invention! As the COVID-19 pandemic taught us, video platforms like Zoom and Webex are excellent ways to connect too.

One other source I want to reference involves what I would call *professional associations*. I didn't list them here because they tend to be highly exclusive. And by exclusive, I mean expensive. So, if you have $10,000 to $100,000 or more to spend on a quarterly retreat and an annual report, then by all means, do it. They are incredibly helpful. I just happen to think that you can get real-time, cutting-edge information for free using the strategies mentioned earlier in this chapter.

Speaking of cutting edge...it does you no good to learn about all the amazing companies and tools that are transforming recruiting if you're not getting involved in the fun! In the next section, I'll introduce a structured and responsible approach to trying out new technologies. This will help you make the right buying decision and can set you up for high adoption and return on investment.

USE STRUCTURED EXPERIMENTATION

True RecOps practitioners are naturally curious. They're early adopters who love to tinker with the latest technologies. As they're learning about all the new tools and talking to sales representatives, they get excited and want to try things. But this can be dangerous. Many companies blindly experiment with new technologies by doing a paid "trial" or half-heartedly playing around with a free version. But because everyone is busy and there is no structure to their experimentation process, the trial fizzles out. The vendor gets frustrated, and the company makes an incorrect assumption that the product doesn't work, when, in fact, maybe it does. It just wasn't given the chance to succeed.

To be clear, I'm 100 percent in favor of trying new tools. It's how I believe we're going to lean forward and fix many of the tedious, error-prone parts of recruiting. But it can't be done haphazardly. Experimenting with new technologies can and should have a structure to it.

Figure 4 is an illustration of a "technology selection funnel." It's a modification of an innovation funnel that you might find in a corporate innovation practice. The process of deciding what technologies to purchase progresses from left to right through stages. In corporate innovation, this is called the "stage gate" approach. Each section of the funnel acts like a gate. To get to the next stage, a new technology has to pass through a set of rules or criteria before it progresses through the gate. This ensures you're making data-driven decisions about which technologies to add to your tech stack and thoughtfully experimenting with them. As the figure demonstrates, you begin by considering a larger collection of technologies, and then you narrow them down through a series of evaluation steps. We'll explore each stage and some recommended gating criteria in this chapter. The five stages are identification, consideration, structured demo, structured pilot, and decision.

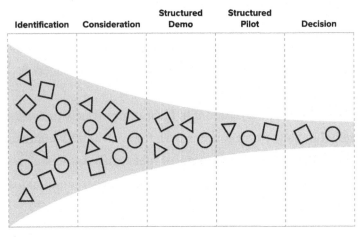

Figure 4

STAGE 1: IDENTIFICATION

This is the top of your experimentation funnel. It's where you take the items from your technology roadmap and your technology education plan and identify them as options you're interested in but aren't taking action on yet. This is where you get to dream big, so put a lot of really cool, audacious technology tools in here that could transform your function, even if you don't know how you will ever afford or implement them.

To help you keep track of the stages in your funnel, I recommend using a tool called Trello. I'm going to go into depth on Trello in the last section of this book. For now, just focus on the concept of a funnel as a structured approach to selecting new technologies. For an example of how Trello can be used to track your experimentation funnel, visit www.recops.org/book/resources or scan the QR code in the resources section at the back of the book.

STAGE 2: CONSIDERATION

At the beginning of this chapter, I introduced the concept of gates. Gates serve the same purpose that they do in real life. They prevent things on one side from getting to the other. In the selection funnel, however, it's not as easy as simply turning a doorknob and walking through. There are rules you should establish to identify when a technology is allowed to pass through to the next stage. Think of the criteria as a checklist. If the tool checks all the boxes, it gets to move from identification to consideration. Here are some criteria you might outline for this stage:

- The tool is in a category of technologies that exists on our roadmap.
- Our team learned about the tool through a podcast, webinar, or conference and feels as though it could solve a problem we have.
- Someone in our industry who knows our needs recommended it to us or validated it.

At this stage, keep the checklist simple. Consideration is

different from identification in that you are committing to a deeper review of a tool. This takes time and effort to coordinate. So, your stage gate checklist should protect that time without being overly restrictive. As you get further down the funnel, your criteria will become more rigorous.

In consideration, you should reach out to the vendor and let them know you are considering their solution. Consider scheduling a brief product overview or maybe even a light demo. The idea is to have an initial conversation about what it does, who the ideal customer is, how the company structures their pricing, and whatever else is important to you. I like to do about one or two of these per week, usually on Friday afternoons. This helps me understand the marketplace better and gives me a mechanism to move tools in and out of my field of view. Otherwise, you just have a big pool of options sitting in your consideration stage. I'm transparent about my process with vendors too. I tell them where they are in my funnel so it sets expectations that I'm not ready to buy. I'm just considering their product.

STAGE 3: STRUCTURED DEMO

If you're adhering to this process, you'll now have a small pool of semi-vetted solutions that sound like they might be a fit, but you still need more information. Much more. The best way to get that information is through a demo. Specifically, a structured demo.

A structured demo is different than the demo a vendor will typically do for you. Normally, if you don't provide guidance, a vendor will just give you a feature demo. This quick tour merely shows you what features the product has and how they work in general scenarios. They'll show you what they want you to see, while failing to mention any shortcomings of the product. What you want to do is provide the exact scenarios the technology will be used for in your environment. Do this prior to scheduling the structured demo. In this way, the vendor can customize the demo for your process, your industry, or whatever else is unique about your situation. If they don't follow the scenario you provide, that should be a red flag.

As you might have deduced, providing a vendor with some structured demo guidelines takes time to prepare. As a result, you'll want to be more protective about which tools you will move into this stage. Here are some recommendations for your checklist:

- We have had an introductory call or initial demo with a representative.
- We have spoken with a current customer of the vendor who validated our use case.
- The tool meets our baseline needs for an existing problem or initiative that exists on our roadmap.
- We have designed a structured demo for the vendor to complete.

- We have specific questions prepared for the vendor.
- The tool doesn't have any deal-breakers (lacks a specific feature, costs too much, doesn't integrate with current systems, etc.).

As you can see, in this stage of the process, you're using more rigorous screening criteria. This ensures that you're doing a more thorough review and limits your exposure to making mistakes. During the structured demo, you should begin to have discussions around price, scope, implementation, security, integrations, and anything else that might be a deal-breaker. If you need help with what questions to ask, meet with your IT or purchasing resources prior to your demo. You may not need them on the call, but it's nice to give them a heads-up, especially if you need to move quickly through the funnel. This is also a good time to start your request for proposal (RFP) process if you have one.

STAGE 4: STRUCTURED PILOT

After a round of structured demos, you will have narrowed down your list of technologies that meet your specific criteria. You should have a really good sense of which products fit your environment, solve your problem, and fit within your budget. Now it's time to design a structured pilot. A structured pilot allows you to get the tool into the hands of your users and play around with it. This will help you further validate if it really works or if it just looks like it works when the vendor is behind the wheel. A structured pilot is typically rolled out in a small part of your organization or for a limited use case. This allows you to sample the technology in your unique environment without requiring you to jump in with both feet.

As part of your pilot plan, you should agree on some key performance indicators (KPIs). KPIs are data-driven goals that you expect the product to hit during the pilot. Some examples include improvements in time, cost, or quality. This allows you to quantify the success of the pilot and helps you make a final decision based on data, not on your gut. Here are a couple of fictitious examples of KPIs you might include in a "chatbot" pilot:

- Less than 10 percent chat abandonment rate.
- Greater than 85 percent of potential applicants who interacted with the bot indicated that it successfully answered their questions.
- At least 20 percent reduction in questions and/or calls to the HR service desk from new hires requiring onboarding assistance.

You should work with your vendor to create realistic KPIs. You don't want to set unrealistic expectations that aren't based on industry baselines.

Your structured pilot should also have a project owner, a defined timeline, and engagement strategies for the team of people you've decided to include in the process. This is typically the role of the person in charge of RecOps. As I mentioned previously, one of the biggest issues I see with pilots is that companies decide to roll them out but fail to communicate the goals to their team. Early in the process, they realize that their team doesn't have the bandwidth or context to engage with the technology. As a result, there is a false negative signal that the technology doesn't work. In reality, the tool probably worked; the team just wasn't properly prepared or freed up to use it.

Finally, you will want to have a budget for pilots. While you might think this is a free service provided by the vendor, it's typically not. Pilots require effort on the part of a vendor, and they should be compensated for it. It also puts your skin in the game, which tends to increase attention on an initiative. Your vendor wants the pilot to work, too, so make sure they are involved in weekly check-ins and update calls. They should be actively involved in helping you prove out your use case during the pilot.

STAGE 5: DECISION

If you've structured your pilot well and it hits all of your expected KPIs, then your decision to buy should be an easy one. To pass through the gate, however, you should establish some criteria similar to what you did for other stages. For example, here are some potential checklist items:

- Pilot is completed with successful achievement of established KPIs.
- Budget is approved and available.
- Purchasing and legal have reviewed and approved a contract.
- IT has completed their security review.
- Recruiting team has provided input and asked questions about the tool.
- Implementation team has been identified.

While this checklist gives you some ideas of what to include in your final selection process, you may have several more hoops to jump through depending on the size of your company and the complexity of your approval process. It's up to you to determine the level of rigor applied to this final step.

The main objective for introducing the technology selection funnel is to help you understand the level of structure your RecOps practice could bring to the selection process. Great selection helps to ensure great adoption, which is the topic that we'll cover next. One important point I'd like to address before I discuss adoption is *the speed* at which a tool can travel through this funnel. I've introduced this concept to some recruiting leaders before whose first reaction was that it would stifle innovation by slowing down the experimentation process. We need to "move fast and break things," they said. While I understand this reaction, the reality is that you can move a new tool through this process in a matter of days if your company enables fast decision-making. It should not slow you down or prevent you from playing with tools you want to explore. In fact, it should open up more options at the top of the funnel and give you a reason (and a format) for trying more of them. In the long run, it will save you time and money by preventing you from making poor choices.

DESIGN ADOPTION STRATEGIES

Using the technology selection funnel is a great example of how RecOps can bring structure to a process that is normally unstructured and reactive. Having a strategy for identification and selection will improve your success rates when investing in new technologies.

But that's only half the job.

If you're going to use technology to transform recruiting, then your RecOps practice should also take responsibility for driving the adoption of your new tools. From my vantage point, this is an area where many companies drop the ball. They buy a new tool but don't have a plan for embedding it into the fabric of their organization. Unfortunately, this approach falls short of delivering the expected results. In the end, the vendor normally gets blamed. But the real reason most technology implementations fail is because there wasn't a plan to make them succeed.

To avoid this situation, your RecOps practitioner, in partnership with your IT/HRIT organizations, should own the full life cycle of your software investments from implementation to replacement. Having a structured plan at each step of the software adoption curve will ensure you address all the challenges you'll encounter when trying to advance your function using tech. The curve has six stages that include implementation, launch, stabilization, optimization, decline, and replacement. Your approach will change at each step of the curve, and the strategies you use will impact adoption levels as shown in Figure 5.

Technology Adoption Lifecycle

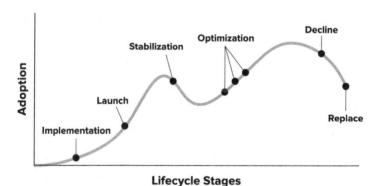

Figure 5

Let's take a brief look at each stage of the adoption curve and review some suggestions on how your RecOps practice can increase your chances of making the most of your technology investments.

STAGE 1: IMPLEMENTATION

The art of implementation could be a book by itself. While I won't go into the depth it deserves in this book, I would be remiss if I didn't provide some thoughts around how to improve an implementation process. If you don't implement correctly, a perfectly good solution will underperform. The most important step to a successful implementation is choosing the right software in the first place. But we already discussed that in the last section of this chapter. To take it to the next level, there are a few things you can do to improve your chances of success.

- **Demand an experienced consultant.** Many software vendors will expose you to their heavy hitters during the sales process. But after the sale is made, you might find yourself being introduced to an inexperienced implementation specialist. I have nothing against a fresh graduate in their first real job, but when you're implementing complex software, you need someone who has done it before and can provide guidance on the product's limitations and possible configurations. Ask to be involved in the selection of your implementation partner, and delay the start of the project if it means you'll get a better resource.
- **Prepare a strong project plan.** Having your own internal project plan is critical. Work with your software vendor to gain alignment on details such as the key milestones, ideal stakeholders, delivery dates, and training

plans. Don't simply accept whatever they give you as the plan.

- **Identify a "system admin."** Any new software needs to have someone who is responsible for its upkeep. This includes tier-one support, training new users, creating new accounts, and liaising with the vendor's help desk. Sometimes this will be your RecOps practitioner. Sometimes it will be someone else on your recruiting team. But the main message here is that it should be someone you trust who also has the bandwidth to commit the time necessary to do it right.
- **Establish adoption metrics.** How will you know if your implementation succeeds? What metrics do you need to hit to achieve the return on investment you were hoping for? Questions like this should be considered before you implement. They will keep you focused on what is important and help drive the activities you want your users to take. Examples might include:
  - Time spent in the tool
  - Number of logins during the week
  - Number of activities performed in the tool
  - Number of positive outcomes using the tool (hires, candidates sourced, interviews scheduled, etc.)

STAGE 2: LAUNCH

While your RecOps practice should have a strong implementation strategy, it's equally important to have a good launch strategy. Launch refers to the activation or rollout of a new technology and the change management that goes along with it. Rolling out anything new inside your recruiting function will be characterized by people who are really excited about the new change and those who are frightened of or opposed to it. Because of this, how you approach a launch could make or break the adoption of a new tool. It's no surprise, then, that a good launch strategy includes a lot of suggestions around structured communication. Here are a few ideas for you to discuss with your RecOps practitioner before you launch:

- **Establish a communication strategy.** Working with your communications team, consider building out a sequence of communications that will both alert and inform your core audience about the implementation. These communications could be segmented for different audiences (users/non-users/executives/hourly) and should include why the new tool is being launched, when it will be launched, how to use it, and who to contact with questions. The earlier you activate communications, the better.
- **Brand your launch.** Along with the communication strategy, some teams have success when branding their launch. For example, a Fortune 500 company that I worked with branded their new ATS launch as a "collaborative hiring system." That word choice signaled two things: the old system was changing, and the new system

would involve a team approach to hiring. This strategy was highly successful because it was clear and used language that non-HR people understood. This approach is much better than announcing an "applicant tracking system upgrade."

- **Stage your rollout.** If you're in a large or complex organization, consider doing your rollout in stages. This might mean releasing it to a planned sequence of geographies or to certain departments before others. This approach allows you to identify problems and share successes that you can refer to as you continue the rest of the rollout. It also prevents you from overwhelming your system admin, who might be on the receiving end of a lot of complaints.

- **Establish an internal help desk.** Even if it's just your system admin, one of the key features of a good launch is having a plan for what happens when things go sideways. Having a clear point of contact for the company to reach out to will serve as an epicenter for the early detection of problems. This will allow you to resolve all the little issues before they become big complaints.

- **Hold daily standup meetings.** In the early stages of a launch, it's important to meet with your core implementation team to monitor how things are going. Getting feedback from users and identifying problems early will help you prevent more issues downstream. I recommend you do this in the first few days and weeks through a daily standup meeting until all of your major issues are resolved.

STAGE 3: STABILIZATION

As the excitement of the launch fades and daily reinforcement dies down, you might find your user adoption in a free fall. This is normal, but you'll need to address it. Stabilization is a time when your RecOps practice should go on the offense to push for long-term habits that will solidify adoption. Here are some proactive measures for consideration:

- **Build a super-user community.** Build a group of people who are committed to the success of the platform and will help you with adoption. Give these individuals early access to upcoming upgrades. Let them play with new features, and provide them with advanced training. If you build an ecosystem of power users, they can help with training and other tier-one support tasks, such as adding new users, running reports, and other simple but time-consuming requests.
- **Activate a training curriculum.** A curriculum is a structured plan for educating a group of people on a specific topic. When executed as a calendar of training activities, it will ensure your users have no excuse for not being proficient with your tools.
- **Monitor adoption metrics.** Once a product launch has stabilized, that's when it's really important to monitor the adoption metrics you established early in the project plan. Looking at them at this stage provides a more realistic perspective. Launch data can give a false sense of value. Depending on what you're measuring, this is

the time to establish baselines. Baselines will help you identify which users are struggling and if your training curriculum is working.

- **Communicate wins.** When you're trying to grow adoption, it's helpful for other users to see how their peers are succeeding with the platform. Whether you distribute it through an intranet, enterprise social network, Slack channel, or email, be sure to share these wins. You should have a few collected from the launch phase.

STAGE 4: OPTIMIZATION

There is no science to knowing when stabilization ends and optimization begins. For most teams, the end of stabilization is marked by the absence of any major system errors that are disrupting the normal operation of the technology. When the help desk has resolved such issues and users have been adequately trained, normally a key member from the vendor's implementation team will fall off, and you'll resume less frequent interactions with them. But that doesn't mean that your efforts should stop. This is the point and time when you continue to go on the offensive and extract additional value out of the tool. This is a core tenet of RecOps, right? Continuous improvement! Here are some ways to do this:

- **Use data to identify adoption issues.** Earlier in this process, you identified some adoption metrics. Now is when they become really important because the data can help you focus your efforts on driving further adoption or optimizing the platform. For example, if you find that no one is using a specific feature you think they should be using, it's a signal that you need to ask your users about the feature. Perhaps it's broken or slow, or they don't know how to use it. Another example might be if you notice the number of emails your users are sending from a CRM is declining. This could mean there is a problem with workflow or usability. This could prompt you to work with the vendor to find a workaround or design a simpler interface. Usage or engagement data can help you optimize your system and, in turn, boost adoption.

- **Stay on top of upgrades.** A good software company will update their platform on a regular basis. Some changes are automatically applied, while others require you to request access. It's important for your RecOps practice to stay on top of these updates so you can take advantage of bug fixes, system enhancements, and even new product extensions. This will extend the life of your product and enhance its everyday usability.

- **Add new modules.** More and more, technology companies are trying to own a broader range of the recruiting process. Sometimes they acquire other companies to add features or products. Sometimes they build them. Either way, it's worthwhile to explore the entire suite of products your vendor offers. This approach could simplify your tech stack, require fewer logins for your users, and streamline reporting. These three benefits can drive additional adoption. This is true only if the entire suite of products is good. Don't add an inferior product just because it's more convenient.

- **Leverage your super users.** By now, your super users are truly super at using your new tool. They know the strengths and weaknesses of the platform and have ideas for how to improve it. Having a regular meeting with this group of people or sending a periodic survey can help you capture ideas that can lead to more improvements. New improvements give frustrated users a new reason to come back into the platform. They also give fans of a tool a reason to keep using it.
- **Pursue integrations.** An integration refers to the connection of one or more systems to another in such a way that data or processes flow between the systems. The theory is that this will improve productivity. It usually does, as long as the integration doesn't break. Integrations are one of the best ways to optimize a workflow. Connecting your ATS to your background check system or an online assessment tool is a good example of this.
- **Influence the product roadmap.** Software vendors, particularly startups, want your input. They often have user communities and conferences where you can suggest product ideas. This is a great way to influence what the company builds next. Being involved at this level is a great way that your RecOps practice can boost optimization.

STAGE 5: DECLINE

In life, all things run their course. In technology, this couldn't be more true. There comes a point in the adoption curve when it becomes counterproductive to continue optimizing a technology. This could be caused by a large global shift in technology (mobile penetration, GDPR, 5G, blockchain, etc.) or a vendor who has stopped updating a product in favor of a newer version. Sometimes it's because you've outgrown the tool through your own corporate growth. Either way, it's important to identify when adoption begins to decline despite your efforts to improve it. It's a signal that a product has reached its peak value.

The primary activity to think about at this stage is beginning to prep your tool for replacement. The biggest consideration is what you're going to do with your data. Your RecOps practitioner should work internally to identify which data you're going to move into the new system. This also includes working with your vendor to figure out how to segment the data and prepare it for extraction. Likewise, your vendor can advise on how to destroy the data that won't be migrated.

STAGE 6: REPLACEMENT

When you have optimized a platform to its fullest extent and it's time to pull the plug, the next step is to identify a replacement. The process of identification and experimentation was outlined earlier in this chapter in Figure 4. Replacing an outdated tool is an exciting time because it gives you the opportunity to take a step back, survey the current landscape, and advance your function through innovative new technology. While this is also a scary proposition, using the principles in this chapter should provide you with a baseline of where to start and how to make a more informed decision.

REFLECTION

I believe that technology will solve many of the problems we experience in our recruiting functions by eliminating the tedious, repetitive tasks that lead to human error. To some degree, I believe technology is what contributes most to the "recruiting is broken" narrative. To fix this, we need to build a capability to manage technology inside our practice of RecOps. We cannot haphazardly select tools and fail to ensure their adoption. Yet we can't stop experimenting with the latest technologies even if they don't fully work yet. It hurts our ability to make industry-wide breakthroughs that we need to improve recruiting.

In the last two chapters, I covered two rather technical topics. These chapters were intentionally detailed to provide some context around the core activities that enable a modern talent acquisition function. I also chose to go deep on those topics to illustrate that you might need a different type of person than you currently have in your organization to do this level of work, or you might need to outsource it. Regardless of how you tackle this work, enabling insights and embracing technology are two fundamentals that, if not mastered, will leave your recruiting function in the dust as the entire world continues to adopt technology at breakneck speeds. While data and technology will help you lean into the future, there is a third fundamental that has the power to separate an average recruiting function from one that is world-class. This fundamental is the ability to layer a consumer-like experience on everything you do for your candidates and your key internal customers. Let's explore this competency further in the next chapter.

CHAPTER 7

Designing Experiences

It's no secret that humans desire positive, memorable experiences. This desire is the number-one driver of the disruptive innovation that we're all witnessing in our daily lives as consumers. The most classic case of this is Uber. If you've ever "hailed" an Uber, you know what I'm talking about. I still remember my first time. It was back in 2012. I received a "free ride" coupon from a hotel I was staying at in New York. I downloaded the app and decided to give it a try. I couldn't believe the sleek, black Cadillac Escalade that rolled up to the curb. When the driver got out, opened my door, and put my luggage in the back, I felt like a rock star! The Uber experience is *exceptional* because it's more than just an improvement over standing on the street corner waving your hand like a crazy person trying to track down a cab. From your mobile phone, you can see who your driver is, what kind of car they're driving, their passenger rating, how soon they will arrive, and what your total cost will be for your trip. It's a dramatically better experience than flagging down a cab.

But Uber is just the tip of the experiential iceberg. This combination of efficiency and experience can be found just about everywhere now. You can order your favorite Sheetz coffee ahead of time through an app and pick it up curbside or have one of our famous made-to-order (MTO) items delivered to your home or office. This wasn't possible just a couple of years ago. You can also reserve seats at the movie theater and jump lines at amusement parks with a "fast pass." Every business on the planet is desperately trying to satisfy the human desire for a better, more convenient experience.

But what are we doing in recruiting? In what ways are we taking cues from this trend and designing experiences for all of our stakeholders? I would argue that we're not doing enough.

In the last several years, an entire industry around "candidate experience" has sprouted up. To be clear, it has made a positive impact on the recruiting industry. But its focus is narrow. Shouldn't it be about the entire experience for all stakeholders, not just candidates? Enabling experiences as a fundamental activity within the practice of RecOps allows you to combine insights and technology to deliver holistic experiences for everyone involved across your hiring process. It's for this reason that designing experiences makes up the third foundational element of a RecOps practice.

In this chapter, I'll review two case studies that illustrate how to combine design with the three fundamentals of RecOps to fix all or part of a recruiting process. In these examples, I'll explore two different tools that you can pull from. Neither is unique to RecOps, but both serve as proven techniques in any industry. They are design thinking and lateral thinking. These examples are also near and dear to my heart, as they come from the time I spent as a RecOps leader at The Hershey Company.

EXAMPLE ONE: FIXING SALES RECRUITING WITH DESIGN THINKING

The term design thinking refers to a method for solving problems using a structured creative process. The earliest forms of design thinking were developed more than thirty years ago to assist architects with the designing of buildings and the planning of urban spaces. In the 1990s, the design firm IDEO made the process hip when they began to market a more formal methodology. Their approach was created to develop innovative new products and services for their blue-chip clients.

While design thinking is typically understood as a tool for designers to create new products, recruiting teams can use it to improve their processes and enhance services. The best time to use it is when you need to create a new process or program from scratch or when you've already tried to optimize something and you're only getting marginal gains. Design thinking can help you make quantum-leap improvements by approaching a project in new and different ways. I experienced this firsthand when I looked at the retail sales recruiting process at The Hershey Company through the lens of RecOps.

Over the years, Hershey's retail sales organization had built a solid recruiting process that seemed to work fine. But when the labor market got stronger and talent was harder to engage, the core metrics started to deteriorate. Application velocity went down, and the interview-to-offer ratio increased. Time-to-fill metrics started to creep up. The net result meant that territories were staying open longer. In the sales world, this translates to lost revenue. It wasn't a great situation to walk into, especially in a sales-led organization like Hershey.

As the new leader of the function, I needed to do something, and I needed to do it fast. The only caveat was I was told that I couldn't change the hiring process because the sales organization wouldn't allow it. So, I did what any RecOps practitioner would do in this situation. I rebelled. I decided to blow the entire process up and rebuild it from scratch. But I would do it *with* the sales team and not *to* the sales team. That's a central theme in the design thinking process. It's a customer-centric approach to solving problems.

Rather than list and describe the steps below, I'm going to illustrate my version of design thinking in the context of solving this challenge. Just keep in mind that depending on who you learn design thinking from or how you deploy it, the exact steps might be different.

STEP 1: DEFINE THE PROBLEM

The problem, as it was described to me, was that retail sales managers needed more and better candidates to fill their open territories. Business leaders defined the problem as a "candidate volume and candidate quality" issue. It's important to note that when your business or HR leaders come to you with a problem, it's not always the *real* problem. It's your job to conduct proper research to get to the root cause and then further define the problem with insights to back it up.

STEP 2: CONDUCT RESEARCH

The first thing I did after receiving the problem statement from sales leadership was to go on an information-gathering binge. I needed to understand the issues from my team's perspective and then from the perspective of sales leaders.

This would allow me to make my own determination of what the real problem was and then begin the hard work of developing a solution.

One of my favorite techniques for conducting research is something that author Steve Blank calls "getting out of the building." Steve is the inventor of the lean startup methodology. His techniques are used by technology startups around the world to build companies based on actual customer feedback instead of hunches. "Getting out of the building" is a phrase he used to encourage startup founders to get out from behind their computers, out of their offices, and physically meet up with the people who are using their software. The idea is to hear directly from the end user what they like and don't like and any ideas they might have to improve the product or service. The lean startup is analogous to RecOps because it's a practice of continuous improvement that has driven massive transformation in the business world.

Taking cues from Steve, I scheduled time to go on "ride-alongs" with retail sales reps to learn about the role. I also scheduled time with managers to learn about their experience with the hiring process. Additionally, I sat in on interviews and talked to new hires to get some feedback about their impressions of the entire experience.

Getting out of the building was by far the most important thing I could have done because it unlocked the insights I needed to identify a few different issues. In design thinking, these insights are called "user stories."

STEP 3: UNCOVER INSIGHTS

User stories are important insights because they represent feedback that comes directly from the people who are involved in the process you're trying to optimize. They also help you articulate point-of-view (POV) statements. These are shorter versions of the user stories that represent patterns you hear over and over during your research. Or they represent the biggest pain points you hear while interacting with the people in your research groups. In this case, here are the POV statements I ended up with:

- **From retail sales hiring managers:** "I need to have all of my territories filled with reps so I can meet my sales goals. I'm spending hours and hours doing phone and face-to-face interviews each week. Recruiting is important, but it's taking too much time away from meetings with customers."
- **From retail sales recruiters:** "We have plenty of good candidates who are applying to our jobs. The problem is, when I'm doing ten to twelve phone screens per day, all the candidates sound roughly the same! So it's hard to know who to send to our managers."
- **From retail sales candidates and new hires:** "The process for an entry-level job was really long. There were a lot of steps, and it involved multiple last-minute travel

requirements. I don't always have the time or money to hop on a plane with less than twenty-four hours' notice."

I also uncovered some hard data from this process that provided me with baseline figures I could focus my team toward improving. One of them was a 92 percent average territory fill rate. This was the percentage of sales territories filled with sales representatives. This was an important revenue-driving metric for our sales executives, so it became a focal point for me in this process.

STEP 4: CREATE A "HOW MIGHT WE" QUESTION

Now that I had some insights from the research process, it was time to create a "how might we" question. This is a question that serves as the starting point for an ideation or brainstorming session. Creating these questions helps you focus your team on a solution based on real insights, not on guesses or unfounded claims from a business leader.

The question that I came up with for this initiative was:

How might we improve our territory fill rate while also giving time back to our managers and improving the overall hiring experience for everyone involved?

This question encapsulated all three of the POV statements that were generated from the research phases. It was an aggressive ask, but design thinking allows you to think big while minimizing risk through a rigorous process. Interestingly, the original problem the sales leadership team brought up—"We need more and better candidates"—did not come up as a core issue during research.

It's also important to note that you don't want to include any potential *solutions* in your "how might we" question. Just frame up an insights-driven, open-ended question that describes your ideal outcome. The last few steps of the design thinking process will deliver the solution.

STEP 5: IDEATION

Ideation, also known as brainstorming, is the part of design thinking that gets the most press. The classic picture of a team of people shouting ideas to a facilitator who is frantically posting sticky notes on a wall is a bit misleading, though. It may lead you to believe that design thinking starts with ideation, when in reality, we don't start talking about generating ideas until Step 5 of 10.

Armed with user-generated insights and a "how might we" question to focus our thinking, I invited a group of people to an ideation session. For a session to be effective, you'll want to invite different types of people to ensure diversity of thought. I invited a small group made up of a recruiter, coordinator, HR manager, recent new hire, and sales manager.

Once we had our group, we focused in on our question and let the ideas flow without judgment. Several ideas we produced were eventually used, and some we discarded. Here are a few:

- Advertise jobs year-round in all markets to build pipelines rather than posting individual jobs when positions become available.
- Use recorded audio interviews to replace phone screens.
- Eliminate the regional director as the final interview step since they rarely reject someone at that stage.
- Reduce last-minute candidate travel issues by using live video for field interviews.
- Replace the "ride-along interview" with an interactive video process that includes work samples and psychometric tests.

Some of these ideas were so bold that we weren't sure sales leaders would buy into them. But that's the beauty of ideation. You get to think big without worrying if it's possible or not. At the end of an ideation session, you choose the most feasible solutions that address your POV statement. The next step is to prototype a simple version of your best solution and go back to your stakeholders to validate that it works.

STEP 6: PROTOTYPE

After I restructured the end-to-end hiring process based on the insights and ideas generated from the design thinking process, I put together a prototype. The prototype involved taking the current seven-step interview process down to four. To do this, I inserted a video interview provider named InterviewStream into the process to replace the initial recruiter phone screen. This recorded video interview would then be used to replace the first phone screen with our sales managers as well. So instead of waiting for a coordinator to stick a phone screen on their calendar during a business workday, the sales manager would simply receive an email with links to a set of videos. The candidates in the videos were chosen for them by a recruiter. This allowed managers to screen candidates at a time that fit their schedule better and gave them more freedom to meet with customers and coach existing team members throughout the day.

To present this completely new process to sales leadership (and get their feedback), I worked with my team to do some mock interviews on the InterviewStream platform so they could see what the experience would look like. I also put together a PowerPoint deck showing what the "before and after" benefits of redesigning the process would be. Then I booked a ticket to fly across the country to speak at a regional sales leaders' meeting in Portland, where I pitched the pro- totype live in front of our head of sales and his direct reports. I honestly thought they were going to throw me out of the room, but after learning it was created using a design thinking process that involved members of their team, they were receptive. Then, after seeing the prototype and learning they would be getting several hours back in their workweek to spend with customers, they wanted to try it. That's where the field testing came in.

STEP 7: TEST

When redesigning a process from the ground up, it's usually best to try it out in one small part of your business. In this case, I picked the Western region because they had the most tech-savvy sales leaders in the country. Their HR business partner was tech savvy too. I had planned to roll out the new process slowly to just a couple of managers over the course of three months, but after a few weeks of using the video interview platform, the entire region wanted to use it. In fact, positive feedback spread so quickly across the country that the other regions started asking for it too.

While this initial test was a big success, it wasn't without its challenges. But a core feature of design thinking is to go through a cycle of refining your solution before you commit to a full launch.

STEP 8: REFINE

In your testing phase, you'll collect feedback and data about how well your initial solution is working. You'll use this information to refine your approach. In this case, one of the key things my recruiting team learned is that you couldn't just send a link to a candidate in an email and expect them to take the video interview—especially in 2012, when video interviewing was really new. We were experiencing a video interview completion rate (VICR) of just 76 percent. This was hurting our manager pass-through rate (MPTR)—a metric we tracked to make sure that our recruiters weren't just lobbing résumés over the fence at our hiring managers. So, we inserted a short five-minute "engagement phone call" from a recruiter to a candidate prior to sending them the video interview link, and our VICR went from 76 percent to 94 percent virtually overnight.

There were some other challenges we had to deal with related to hiring managers who were resistant to change, but we partnered with our HR managers to step up our education program for them. Over time, their concerns went away.

STEP 9: LAUNCH

In this rare case in which the solution was so well received, the launch of the new process wasn't much of a launch at all. But that's a sign that you used design thinking in its most optimal form. We did, however, need to select a date when the old process would be closed down and we would only use the new video-enabled process moving forward. That date happened two months ahead of schedule.

STEP 10: ONGOING REFINEMENT

Design thinking is an iterative process. The act of listening to your customers and refining your solution never stops. Over the years, the Hershey retail sales recruiting team honed the new process into a well-oiled machine that was delivering an average territory fill rate that exceeded 99 percent. Previously, it hovered around 92 percent. That means throughout the year, almost 100 percent of territories were filled, which directly resulted in higher revenues for the company.

Thinking back to the original "how might we" question, we refined the other areas targeted for improvement as well. The new process gave back a significant amount of time to sales managers. The candidate experience was also improved through the elimination of two unnecessary interviews. In addition, the reduction of last-minute travel requests saved Hershey a lot of money on interview travel costs as well.

Overall, this project was viewed as a major success by sales leadership and proved that design thinking was a great way to take a tired, old process and dramatically improve the experience of everyone involved. And it reinforced how the combination of insights, technology, and experience—the three fundamentals of RecOps—can be combined to spark the transformation.

EXAMPLE TWO: USING LATERAL THINKING TO FIX THE JOB FAIR EXPERIENCE

In the previous example, a formal approach was taken to transform a recruiting process using design thinking. This was a planned, strategic process that fit nicely into our RecOps practice. Sometimes, however, your practice needs to enable a faster cycle of innovation to fix problems as they arise. Fortunately, when you build a RecOps practice, you're building a muscle that powers problem-solving whenever you need it.

A year after implementing the new retail sales recruiting process at Hershey, things were going pretty well. But in March of that year, I got an urgent email from my VP of talent with the subject line: "See me immediately re: Retail Sales." Historically, urgent emails like this meant that something big had gone wrong!

When he and I finally connected, he explained to me that Hershey's CEO was the new president of the board of an organization called Enactus. Enactus is a nonprofit organization dedicated to developing the next generation of entrepreneurial leaders. They host a conference and competition each year for university students. Our campus recruiters and sales leaders always attended, but it was never a great place to recruit talent because it took place in May. By that time of year, most attendees had already secured internships and full-time jobs.

The urgency around this situation was that our CEO was speaking at the event and wanted to "make a splash" with our booth at the conference. Because the event wasn't a great source of hires, we typically dialed back our booth for the conference. We normally just had a couple of tables and a few bowls of candy for anyone who stopped by to chat with us. Now that our CEO was the president of the board, we needed to show up in a more professional way. But I wasn't quite sure what he meant when he said to "make a splash," and neither was my VP. But we both agreed that when he visited the booth at the event, he'd better be impressed!

FROM ONE INDUSTRY TO ANOTHER

To begin the process of "making a splash," I put together a small team. It consisted of my graphic designer, Brad Fuhrman, whom I'll talk about later in this book, and our campus recruiter, Colleen Sheibley. On top of the vague directive, the biggest challenge we faced was that it was currently March, and the conference was in May. That meant we had about two months to design and build a unique job fair experience. Usually, job fair booth design takes several months. It also costs tens (sometimes hundreds) of thousands of dollars, and we had a budget of exactly zero dollars. Since this wasn't an item we'd budgeted for at the beginning of the year, we would have to do this project with no money or find it from somewhere else.

Having tools like design thinking in your optimization repertoire are a must for any RecOps practice. Sometimes when you don't have enough time (or money) but you still need to create a unique experience, you have to steal ideas from other industries and apply them to your own. Since HR typically lags behind other industries in the adoption of new technologies, there are numerous opportunities to create modern solutions that are years ahead of their time. All you have to do is use a little "lateral thinking" to stimulate ideas.

Lateral thinking is a way of solving problems by developing different and original strategies rather than using traditional or expected methods. Some say the ability to do this is a gift. I think it can be learned if you just train your brain to look for ideas everywhere you go.

About thirty minutes into the first meeting with my team, we realized that redesigning the booth was not going to be an option. We cycled through a bunch of initial ideas, but none of them felt like they satisfied the "make a splash" directive. For example, we discussed using a projector to play Hershey commercials on a big screen in the booth. We thought about flying the Hershey Kiss character to the event, so they could dance around and pull candidates into our booth. We even thought about setting up a fake store with Hershey products on shelves and creating a checkout counter where students had to pay for their candy with a résumé. It was clever, but it wasn't the big idea we were looking for.

That's when I remembered my recent trip to a local convenience store.

AN INTRODUCTION TO AUGMENTED REALITY

Ideas come from the craziest of places. I was standing about twelve people deep in line at the convenience store with a hot cup of coffee in my hand. It was January 2013. I was already running late for work, so I wasn't too happy that the line was so long. As it turned out, the Mega Millions lottery was on its way to an all-time high of over $300 million. While the people in front of me were loading up on tickets, my attention was called to a point-of-sale display sitting on the floor. It was a promotional display run by 7-Up, a popular carbonated beverage. To win the prize, they wanted you to download their augmented reality app. I don't even remember what the prize was, but this was the first time I had seen a real application of augmented reality in any environment. Keep in mind this was early 2013. Augmented reality wasn't even a thing back then. I would argue that even now, in 2021, it still hasn't realized its potential. While 2013 might seem like a long time ago in a book that touts the use of modern strategies, stay with me. There's a two-part lesson here. One is about taking risks with bleeding-edge technologies, and the other is about using lateral thinking to apply ideas from another industry to your own.

If you're not familiar, augmented reality, or AR for short, is a technology that uses the camera on a mobile device and something called object recognition to overlay a digital experience on top of something in the real world. A really simple example of this is the floating digital enhancements you can make to your face in the Snapchat app. Those are called filters. In the case of 7-Up, the use case was designed to get consumers to opt in to a promotion. Intrigued (and with nothing better to do), I set my cup of coffee on the floor and downloaded the app. When it was done, I pointed the camera of my iPhone at the "trigger image." The trigger image is the name given to the object that your camera will recognize to trigger some sort of digital experience. When I did this, it nearly took my breath away. Right there on my phone, I watched the trigger image come to life. A man danced around my screen holding a can of 7-Up, and a video played that told me all about the promotion. This was the first time I had ever seen AR in action. I made note of the company that built the app, told a few people about it that day, and then forgot about it until the day of our "make a splash at the job fair" meeting.

As we kicked around bad ideas for our job fair booth, we had one core principle written on a flipchart. It read, "Design a unique human experience." Keeping this in mind, we began to talk about how the job fair experience was definitely not a great human experience. In fact, job fairs have actually gotten worse over time. Innovation has mainly come in the form of bigger booths with more creative uses of space—like the use of couches and Airstream trailers, for example. The concept is still the same: attendees line up, talk to a company rep for two or three minutes, hand over their résumé, and walk off with a paper brochure. If they're lucky, they'll get a call back later that day to interview in a makeshift, curtain-walled office flanked by three other candidates doing the same thing.

In this environment, candidates don't have an opportunity to engage with the company culture, understand the direction of the business, or clearly see the reasons why they should join. The entire process is designed around efficiency, not experience.

Leveraging this belief about job fairs, I asked my team the following question:

How might we bring The Hershey Company employment brand to life and reinvent the in-booth candidate experience with measurable hiring outcomes?

I shared with them my recent 7-Up AR moment, and it resulted in the sketch you see in the following figure. This was a design thinking shortcut that we had to take due to lack of time, but it checked off all the boxes we had in terms of our objectives. And just like that, we were off and running with a novel idea.

AR Wall

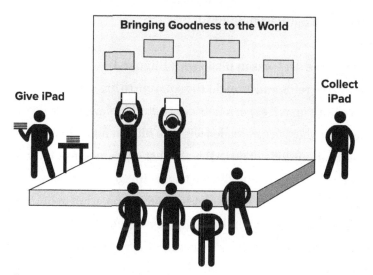

Figure 6

REINVENTING THE JOB FAIR EXPERIENCE

In 2013, AR had never been used at a job fair. But we hypothesized that we could use the concept to create an experience that would excite the college-age demographic while informing them of the key pillars of our employee value proposition. During my brief interaction with AR at the convenience store, I made note of the company that built the 7-Up experience. They were called Blippar. At the time, Blippar was a UK-based company, and they were only a couple of years old. That allowed us to partner with them at a really low cost in exchange for some free press from a big brand like Hershey. To save time and additional money, we recycled preapproved content from our corporate communications team and did all the design work in-house through our designer, Brad.

Once the deal was in place with Blippar, Brad and Colleen took the reins and brought the solution to life in record time. We built an AR experience where students would be given an iPad that was preloaded with the Blippar app. They would start at one side of an "AR wall" that contained five trigger images. When scanned, each trigger image would bring one pillar of the Hershey employee value proposition to life. As they navigated down the path, they watched commercials, learned about Hershey's sustainability programs, and, as a final step, provided their contact information in a single click. No résumé exchanges. No awkward two-minute speed interviews. No couches. Just an engaging, tech-enabled, unique human experience.

While the solution was certainly cool, it was effective too. The AR experience created a buzz throughout the conference. There were lines queued up to use it, and we captured a significantly higher number of contacts than ever before.

In addition, we made more hires at that event than in all previous attempts.

The best part was when our CEO and chief human resources officer (CHRO) visited the booth, they were blown away! Mission accomplished. And we used the three fundamentals of RecOps to deliver results. We used insights and technology with a proven technique called lateral thinking to design a more engaging human experience.

To see the finished version of the AR job fair booth, visit https://recops.org/book/resources.

REFLECTION

In Part 1 of this book, I defined what RecOps is. In Part 2, I transitioned to provide examples of the activities that drive transformation. I defined those activities as enabling insights, embracing technology, and designing experiences.

It's important to note that the challenges you face will be different than those described in these chapters. You'll choose to fix different parts of your function to meet your unique business needs. But if you focus on the three fundamentals when building your RecOps practice, you'll set yourself up to design a modern talent acquisition function that is capable of standing up to any problem that exists in today's or tomorrow's recruiting environment.

At this point in the book, though, you might be thinking, *Who the heck is going to do all this RecOps work?* It's a natural question. And an important one. Perhaps *the most* important one. Because in order to build and sustain your RecOps practice, you need to have someone with the right skills, experience, and ambition in place to drive a continuous approach. This person is what I like to call the RecOps practitioner, and they are the focus of Part 3 of the book.

The RecOps Practitioner

CHAPTER 8

The Tony Stark Model

Recruiting jobs as we know them today will cease to exist in less than ten years. Maybe five. Possibly three. Some jobs will simply change. Others will disappear. That debate is over.

The sooner we accept that, the sooner we can prepare ourselves and our functions for this transition and start an action plan to get out ahead of it.

The reason some roles will *change* dramatically is because of technology. The reason some roles will *disappear* is because the people who occupy them will fail to evolve their skills to account for a more technology-facilitated recruiting environment. A good example of this is happening in another industry right now: your local grocery store.

About two years ago, I started to notice my supermarket piloting self-checkout stations. You've probably noticed them too. Back then, there were one or two stations. Last week, I counted ten.

There are almost as many self-checkout lanes as there are human-operated ones now. And since the automated stations tend to be glitchy, grocery stores need someone who can fix them in real time to keep the lines moving. This need makes the self-checkout cashier different than your run-of-the-mill cashier. They have a more modern skillset.

I spoke to the general manager of my local grocery store, who filled me in on how technology is impacting their talent strategy. She told me that, at first, they tried to move traditional cashiers over to the self-checkout area. That strategy failed miserably. The traditional cashier lacked the ability to multitask in a more complex, faster-moving environment. They didn't have the troubleshooting skills to fix the computers when they broke down, and they struggled to maintain a friendly demeanor during peak checkout volume.

To combat this challenge, the store invested in upskilling their high-potential staff. In partnership with their kiosk vendor, they developed a training program that helped tremendously. Moving forward, I was told the type of cashier they hire today is completely different.

Today, instead of hiring someone who can count money and scan grocery items, they're hiring people who can solve problems, troubleshoot issues, interact with customers socially, and stay friendly under fire. They also look for people who take an active interest in learning new technology inside and outside of work.

The results have been amazing.

Now, a single "modern" cashier can handle ten lanes of customers or more. While this certainly has a labor cost savings attached to it, an added value is that stores can handle traffic spikes much better, which leads to a more efficient experience for customers.

In addition to cost savings and faster checkout options, kiosks have had an impact on employee engagement. The store is able to move modern cashiers back and forth from manual to automated checkout lanes to break up the monotony of a shift. They can also move them to a completely different task somewhere else in the store. This has shown initial gains in staff retention, which is a big win in the retail and grocery industry.

If these positive results continue to scale without a dip in customer satisfaction, the store manager estimates that within three years, approximately 80 percent of the checkout lanes will be self-service.

In the recruiting industry, most of our professionals are like the traditional cashier. We have recruiters, coordinators, and managers who are friendly and can follow a defined process. But there aren't very many who know how to manage a technology integration, set up a chatbot sequence, or analyze recruitment marketing data to uncover wasted advertising spend. As we enter a more technology-enabled work environment, these are the skills of the future. And these are the skills that form the bedrock necessary to transform your recruiting function from traditional to a more modern practice leveraging the principles of RecOps.

WHO IS YOUR TONY STARK?

The evolution of the grocery store cashier follows a trend that I like to call the Tony Stark Model. Tony Stark is the main character in a Marvel franchise movie called *Iron Man*. By day, Tony is the CEO of a weapons defense company. By night, he plays the role of a superhero who wears a technology-enabled, armored suit that turns him into Iron Man. When aided by technology, he has superhuman strength, augmented reality vision, and advanced weapons capabilities. His suit is also connected to a network so he can access the data that he needs to find bad guys and exploit their weaknesses.

When we apply this concept to the recruiting industry, many leaders and influencers are predicting a future in which recruiters are tech-enabled like Tony Stark. They will take on a more evolved role similar to the modern grocery store cashier. They will maintain a much-needed human presence throughout the hiring process but will supercharge their ability to find, engage, and convert talent using technology. Perhaps they'll be able to do the work of four or five recruiters or sourcers. While we're still a few years away from mass adoption, I don't think the concept is unrealistic. However, to make this a reality, you have to ask yourself the following question:

> **Who on my recruiting team is going to select, implement, integrate, and optimize game-changing processes, programs, and technologies that enable a Tony Stark–like future?**

Do you have someone on your team who can do this? Or are you cobbling resources together from other departments or via consultants?

Not to geek out too much over the movie, but it's important to note that Tony is the one who builds the suit, programs it, and fixes it when it breaks. He doesn't just buy one from the Iron Man store, put it on, and become a superhero. He has a different skillset that allows him to customize and enable this technology to be put into practice. This is a unique attribute of a RecOps practitioner. They are the missing link to operationalizing the processes, programs, and technologies that will change our industry.

If we want to change the face of our function and improve our industry, we can no longer continue to dream about what "could be." It's time for us to start tinkering in the lab and playing with the tools that could eventually lead us to a Tony Stark–like future. To do that, we have to develop an industry of RecOps practitioners who are skilled at doing this and unleash them on projects that will optimize everything we do. I strongly advocate that most recruiting departments build these capabilities in-house. In the next chapter, I'll discuss why most companies are missing the mark today and what to do about it.

CHAPTER 9

The Multipurpose Recruiter

If you were the owner of a professional baseball team, would you want your star player to be the pitcher and the third baseman? Would you want that person keeping the team stats and serving as the vice president of marketing? Would you also want them managing the team? Of course you wouldn't. That's a terrible use of a valuable resource! You're also highly unlikely to find someone who has all the skills required to do such a wide variety of specialized tasks, let alone have the time to do them.

But if this scenario sounds so silly, why do we do this to our recruiting staff?

Why do we ask them to carry a full load of requisitions, plus be the ATS administrator, plus manage the social media accounts, plus develop the interviewer training program, plus select the new background check vendor, plus coordinate university recruiting trips?

These tasks fall within the scope of a recruiting function, but like the baseball example, they require different skills and take your valuable resources away from what they should really be doing: engaging top talent and delivering an amazing hiring experience.

This strategy is the most common approach that recruiting leaders are using to deal with the wide array of challenges coming at them from all angles. They spread their tasks and projects among their recruiters or leaders who are not trained in the art of managing projects, building programs, or implementing technologies. Surprisingly, recruiting teams seem to relish this extra work. They are proud to tell you about the high volume of tasks they're juggling. There is a culture in the recruiting industry whereby a badge of honor is given to individuals and teams who work long hours, carry huge requisition loads, and do the jobs of two or three people.

But does it have to be this way? Do we have to overextend ourselves to prove our value to an organization? I think not. And it's clearly not working.

I would argue that it's this bravado that prevents recruiting teams from transforming their function from a collection of disjointed experiences and outdated technologies to one that delivers a seamless experience across the recruiting supply chain. This scenario also leads to a stressed-out recruiter who struggles to keep up with their requisition load. This negatively impacts the candidate and hiring manager experience. It also perpetuates the endless cycle of a broken hiring process and adds fuel to the "recruiting is broken" fire.

So back to the question I asked earlier: why do we do this to our recruiting staff?

Well, the simple answer is that recruiting leaders struggle to obtain approval for the dedicated headcount required to focus on non-recruiting, continuous improvement tasks. In the absence of headcount, we frame these tasks as "developmental opportunities" for our top performers and spread them out across the team. While this can truly be great development, the term "developmental" implies that you are preparing your staff for a specialized role at some point in the future. In reality, though, this strategy typically doesn't lead to anything other than taking on more work for a person who demonstrates the ability to juggle several tasks at once.

To be clear, I understand why many organizations do this. I've worked in resource-constrained environments where I had to wear many hats too. But these experiences were painful and resulted in work I wasn't proud of. I personally contributed to the "recruiting is broken" mantra. To achieve operational excellence and prepare for a more technology-enabled future, we'll need to break this cycle and start adding resources dedicated to streamlining operations and optimizing our functions in a deliberate and ongoing way. But it's not as simple as just adding headcount or repurposing an existing team member. It has to be the *right person*, capable of transforming your function from the inside out.

CHAPTER 10

The Modern RecOps Practitioner

A modern RecOps practitioner is someone who can enable the model I described in Chapter 2. I've included the model again here as a reminder of the importance of RecOps as a continuous improvement engine. A RecOps practitioner understands that recruiting is a living system, and they live to connect the dots between the clarity of your strategy, the fundamentals of RecOps, and the transformation of your function. They represent the Tony Stark of your department. But who are they? What skills do they have? And what, specifically, should you put them in charge of?

The RecOps Model

STRATEGY	OPERATIONS	RECRUITING	DATA	RECOPS
Mission	Processes	Kickoff	Cost	Data Analysis
Vision	Programs	Sourcing	Quality	Technology Enablement
Strategy	Technology	Advertising	Speed	
Goals	Compliance	Screening	Volume	Experience Design
Priorities	Budget	Scheduling	Experience	
	Training	Interviewing	Feedback	Continuous Improvement
	Reporting	Offers	Surveys	
	Calendars	Onboarding	KPIs	

Enhancements feed back into the system driving continuous improvement & transformation.

Figure 1

In preparation for writing this book, I reviewed hundreds of job descriptions and talked to many practitioners who are currently sitting in RecOps roles. As expected, there was a tremendous amount of variety in how roles were defined at each company; however, some patterns emerged too. One interesting pattern is that your RecOps practitioner doesn't need to come from your recruiting function. In fact, some of the best practitioners I've worked with didn't come from the talent acquisition ranks. My current RecOps leader at Sheetz, Mara Lytle, for example, came from our commercial real estate development function. At Cielo, one of my star technology-enablement consultants, Rebecca Volpano, was a former category development manager for Victoria's Secret. Neither of their backgrounds would be considered "ideal" for someone who optimizes a recruiting function. And yet they excel. Why is that?

The common denominator of a talented RecOps practitioner

is that they need to be uncomfortable with the status quo. They have to see every process, program, and technology as if they are all in beta just waiting to be optimized. They need to view transformation as a practice, not as a one-time event. Mara and Rebecca have this in spades!

Now, just because you have a dedicated resource assigned to recruiting operations or talent ops, that doesn't mean you have a practice of RecOps on your hands. You have to properly define the practice and design the role to enable the right outcomes. You also need to ensure the person you put in the role has the right skills to advance your function.

In the remainder of this chapter, I'll summarize the most common responsibilities that repeat as themes across all industries. This should be helpful as you think about hiring someone to build out your RecOps practice, or, if you already have someone, it will help you define their role more clearly. To begin, let's take a look at the most critical responsibilities, a brief explanation of each one, and some of the skills required to be effective. These are written as they might sound in a job description. If you'd like to see multiple examples of good RecOps job postings, visit www.recops. org/book/resources or scan the QR code in the resources section of the book.

In the next section, we'll explore what to look for when building these capabilities in-house. If you don't think you'll be able to do this in-house, stay with me. In the last chapter, we'll look at alternative ways to carry out RecOps activities without the need for additional headcount.

WHAT DOES A RECOPS PRACTITIONER DO?

In my study of recruiting organizations around the world, I found a large variety of job titles that are essentially doing the same thing. Some common ones that I encountered include:

- Manager of Recruiting COE
- Recruiting Operations Manager
- Talent Ops Analyst
- Manager of Talent Acquisition Innovation
- RecOps Lead

As an industry, we've been really creative with the job titles for roles that are essentially designed to perform the same task: recruiting transformation. To be clear, I hope that someday we can all rally around the term RecOps, similar to the way that a sourcer, an employment brand specialist, and a recruiting coordinator mean really clear things to everyone in our industry today. I believe if we consolidate our nomenclature, we can all get aligned around the core duties and start standardizing (and sharing) best practices in a unified way. In this section, I'll cover the most common and critical duties that have been attached to these transformational roles.

1. ENABLING INSIGHTS

The RecOps practitioner automates data extraction from multiple sources to build dashboards and data sets that enable insights, lead metrics strategies, and run ad hoc reports to diagnose issues.

Today, most recruiting organizations have someone on the team who runs reports on a weekly basis. Typically, they have a good handle on how to use Excel or Google Sheets. While these are good skills to have, many companies are moving beyond tools like these. The main reason is because they limit an organization's ability to combine data sets into actionable dashboards and data warehouses. A more advanced approach also prevents sending reports that are outdated as soon as they're emailed to the end user. Fortunately, cloud-based reporting tools have enabled the ability to automate and manipulate data from all of your recruiting technologies into a single store of data. In Chapter 5, Enabling Insights, I covered how to do this in detail. While a modern RecOps practitioner doesn't need to be a data scientist, they should bring an understanding of how to harness more advanced tools that transcend the standard Excel-based reporting that is so pervasive in recruiting functions all over the world.

The ability to design visuals that tell a story is also an important skillset. Your RecOps practitioner should be familiar with wireframing tools such as Basalmiq, UXPin, or even Visio. These tools allow them to create mockups of dashboards and other visualizations to uncover the best approach to present your data.

2. TECHNOLOGY ENABLEMENT

The RecOps practitioner owns and optimizes technology stacks, drives adoption and usability to help team members get the most out of their tools, and manages vendor relationships.

The ability to make use of modern technology represents the single biggest opportunity to optimize your function. But if you talk to most recruiting leaders, they will admit they are grossly underutilizing their existing tools. In the next breath, they'll ask you what new tools they should be using. This classic case of underutilization and chasing the latest shiny toy is an issue that stems from not having someone who is responsible for optimizing your technology investments. To remedy this situation, you should look to bring strong technical expertise into your RecOps practice.

RecOps professionals don't need to have programming skills, but they should be able to hold their own with vendors and internal technology resources. Ultimately, they will be the person who enables a Tony Stark–like experience for recruiters, so they'll need technical knowledge and strong project management skills, such as requirements-gathering, process design, and vendor management. The ability to integrate systems is also important. Connecting systems can help streamline workflows and allow for the blending of siloed data. Post-implementation adoption skills are critical too. A RecOps practitioner should be scheduling checkpoints, monitoring usage metrics, and conducting trainings to ensure the technology is up to date and adoption levels are high.

There is a lot of ground to cover under the topic of technology enablement. Many larger organizations will solve for this by hiring a recruiting systems lead or talent acquisition technology lead. This role tends to be a specialized role and might be different than someone who owns other RecOps responsibilities. However you decide to address this essential element, make it a priority to enhance your ability to build a strong, connected technology stack. Your RecOps practitioner should help you extract value out of what you currently own and implement the advanced tools you need to embrace the future.

3. EXPERIENCE DESIGN

The RecOps practitioner builds a consumer experience layer on top of core services to ensure that candidates and internal customers have an easy and enjoyable time engaging with processes.

A consumer-driven experience places an end user on a pedestal when designing products and services. Companies like Apple and Disney sparked a revolution in this space. But recruiting departments often lose sight of creating experiences when things get busy. Which is all the time, right? In the midst of overwhelm, teams default to creating processes that make it easier for them to operate but fail to account for the needs of their customers. In the increasingly competitive world we live in, improving our focus on our end user is a key to improving our internal operations and differentiating our employment brand externally. In a modern recruiting function, this unique responsibility lands squarely in the lap of a RecOps professional.

Creating amazing experiences used to be difficult. There weren't many case studies. But thanks to organizations like the Talent Board, the idea of improving the candidate experience has been elevated within the enterprise recruiting community. Fortunately, this has paved the way for recruiting leaders to think more broadly about how they can apply this thinking to other areas of their function as well. But like other ideas in this chapter, it begs the question, "How?" How do we create better experiences? The answer is by first placing an emphasis on experience design in your hiring process via a structured RecOps practice. This can be done by applying techniques and skills that come from the design industry. For example, the capability to run design-thinking sessions can help develop breakthrough solutions that are centered on your users. We covered this in Chapter 7, Designing Experiences. Traditional process-mapping skills are okay too, but they typically focus on the steps of the process, not the user experience.

The field of user experience (UX) design also holds numerous proven methodologies that can improve the way teams think about delivering their services. You may not have the resources to hire a dedicated UX designer, but building the capabilities to use some of their tools will drive better outcomes for your customers. In summary, your RecOps practice should place an emphasis on taking our clunky technologies and our convoluted processes and putting a melty, buttery layer of experience on top.

4. RESEARCH AND INNOVATION

The RecOps practitioner routinely scans the market for new ideas, builds a process for turning ideas into reality, and pushes the boundaries of what is possible.

If you think about RecOps as an engine for continuously improving your function, you'll understand that this engine needs fuel. One such fuel comes in the form of ideas. Lots of them. How (and how often) you generate ideas is important too. So, another fuel for routinely improving your function is having a process to generate more ideas.

Think of it this way. When you have a problem to solve,

do you just kick some ideas around in a meeting, hold a brainstorming session, or phone a friend? Or do you have a structured way of generating ideas to help you identify solutions that will improve your function? These solutions could be a new piece of technology or a redesigned process, for example. To make a long-term impact on your function, you would be doing yourself a favor if you have a defined way to do this. Your RecOps practitioner should help you get there.

Putting research and innovation together requires the ability to routinely scan the market for new ideas and apply them responsibly. I use the term "responsibly" because the reckless implementation of ideas just creates chaos. We're trying to avoid that as much as possible.

5. PROCESS OPTIMIZATION

The RecOps practitioner builds, documents, and optimizes processes to ensure efficiencies in speed, cost, quality, and experience across a wide variety of hiring activities.

The ability to optimize parts of a recruiting function is a core competency for a RecOps professional. As a result, process optimization is a critical responsibility. To do this, your RecOps resource needs to have a modern skillset that includes exposure to or expertise in methods such as process mapping, design thinking, Six Sigma, kaizen, growth hacking, and others used to optimize business processes. RecOps practitioners use these methods to systematically improve speed, cost, quality, and experience metrics in a positive direction.

6. PROJECT MANAGEMENT

The RecOps practitioner owns the setup, management, and delivery of recruiting projects.

Projects in a recruiting function can range anywhere from highly complex technology implementations to the simple act of rewriting some hiring policies. The variety can be quite staggering. For this reason, one of the first responsibilities that a recruiting leader assigns to a RecOps role is project management. And rightfully so. Many activities in a function that need to be improved are best packaged up and run like a project.

In the past, to be a successful project manager you needed to have great organizational skills, the ability to communicate effectively, and the right balance of tact and tenacity to push projects through to completion. Today, however, the skills required have grown. In addition to the classic characteristics mentioned above, project managers should have exposure to different methods of running a project, such as Waterfall, Agile, and Kanban. It's not unusual for different methods to be used by different teams within an organization. It's also not unusual for multiple methods to be used during the same project!

Tools are important today too. A project manager is often relied upon to set up and maintain modern project tracking software such as Trello, Monday, or Asana. I'll introduce one of these tools later in the book as my favorite way to manage various RecOps activities.

7. PROGRAM MANAGEMENT

The RecOps practitioner develops, manages, and optimizes hiring programs to ensure they are thoughtfully launched and closely managed to ensure successful outcomes.

Programs within a recruiting function can enable special capabilities. For example, a referral program can enable an entire company to participate in the sourcing of talent. An internal mobility program can establish a clear path for employees to grow their careers. The value of having great programs is undeniable. But they're not easy to build or maintain. With the number and importance of programs rising every year, a dedicated resource is required.

The skill of building a program is different than managing a program after it is launched. Creating a program might require creativity or the ability to cobble together best practice examples obtained from peers. Rolling a program out requires planning, communication, and change-management skills. Video or graphic design capabilities could be valuable in this endeavor too. The key to deriving value from your programs is what happens after they're launched. Far too often, companies roll out a program or implement a technology and think the job is done. But the real value of a program comes from designing checkpoints and regular meetings to review progress, metrics, and problems. This is a central theme in a RecOps practice.

8. TRAINING AND INSTRUCTIONAL DESIGN

The RecOps practitioner uses data to develop training materials that elevate the understanding and usability of processes, programs, and technologies while leveling up teams and key stakeholders.

It's unrealistic to think everyone on your recruiting team has the same level of knowledge about any topic. Each person has a different understanding of how to interview, how to source talent, how to use an ATS, etc. But wouldn't you agree it's important for your entire team to be knowledgeable about recruiting best practices or even baseline techniques if they're early in their career? If so, then why don't most recruiting functions have a curriculum for leveling up their team? The answer is because it's not a capability that is common in most recruiting organizations. Learning is often left to chance, but it doesn't have to be.

Making instructional design and training a responsibility within your RecOps practice will accelerate your initiatives and help you embed all of the improvements you're going to make to your function. These capabilities shouldn't be directed only at your internal team. Your other customers should benefit too. For example, your candidates want to be educated about your hiring process. They also want to know what to do when they reach the onboarding stage. Your hiring teams also need help. They only engage with your process periodically, so they need easy-to-use refresher courses to ramp up quickly in a fast-moving process.

To be successful at this, a RecOps practitioner doesn't need to have experience teaching or spending time in a learning and development (L&D) function, especially if they partner with L&D or an external partner. But it does help if they can identify gaps in knowledge within a population and develop a list of educational materials that will bridge those gaps. Once this learning curriculum is designed, the ability to develop materials becomes important. These materials could come in the form of short videos, simple one-page documents, or presentations.

CHAPTER 11

Avoiding Overload

If you're planning to develop an in-house RecOps practice and staff it with a modern RecOps practitioner, one of the biggest mistakes you can make is overloading this person with too much work. By adding too much to a RecOps practitioner's plate, you run the risk of overwhelming the very person you're entrusting to optimize your function!

Below are some examples of responsibilities I found in my research that could potentially distract your resource from having the most impact. I'm not saying these duties can't work in your specific situation; just be careful adding these responsibilities to an already-full plate.

MANAGING RECRUITMENT COORDINATORS

Most recruiting operations roles today are born out of a need to manage administrative things like interview scheduling, background checks, and onboarding. While it's true these tasks have a lot of moving parts, they tend to be admin-heavy activities that require a strong attention to detail. As a result, they can be a huge time-suck for a RecOps practitioner who also has the responsibility of building and optimizing programs, processes, and technologies. For this reason, managing recruitment coordinators should be a role more closely tied to the core recruiting workflow. The idea that scheduling and onboarding are administrative tasks that should be separated from the core recruiting workflow can cause a disconnect between a hiring team and the coordinator team. This is one of the biggest complaints I hear from recruiting leaders whose coordinators are located in a remote shared-services function, handling scheduling and onboarding. If done really well, this model *can work*. But the level of continuity required in the handoffs between recruiters, managers, and candidates makes it difficult. By removing the management of coordinators from a RecOps practitioner's plate, it frees up their ability to perform the other core duties I've outlined in the previous chapter. The ideal situation is that someone else manages the coordinators, or you promote a coordinator to a lead coordinator who handles the day-to-day escalations that typically bog a manager down. After you do this, your RecOps practitioner can focus on optimization and work closely with the team to streamline their processes and enable helpful tools that will make them more efficient.

MANAGING THE RECRUITING BUDGET

One of the biggest outcomes a RecOps practice or person must drive is financial optimization. To do this, they need to have close knowledge of the recruiting budget and how funds are spent. But that doesn't mean they should own or manage the budget. The monthly reconciliation process has a tendency to bog down even the most financially savvy person. As a workaround, a RecOps lead could obtain intimate knowledge of the budget through regular meetings with finance to discuss areas of the budget that are running high and brainstorm some ways to trim costs or shift priorities that could have a positive financial impact on the function.

RECRUITING AGENCY MANAGEMENT

One of the most common duties you'll see on a recruiting operations job description is vendor management. Sometimes that means technology vendor, and sometimes that means recruiting agency vendor. Sometimes it means both. I think these two types of vendor groups should have different owners. The natural owner for your stack of technology vendors is whoever heads up your RecOps or recruiting technology practice. This person will be a key force in driving your technology roadmap, so they should own the relationships.

Now, the opposite is true with recruiting agencies or headhunters. Since your recruiters are typically working with them on a regular basis, it makes sense for a recruiting manager or director to own the relationships. That said, a RecOps practice can also be leveraged to enable better partnerships, so they should be involved in some way. For example, they could develop a preferred vendor program and online portal to identify, monitor, and reward your best recruiting partners.

EMPLOYMENT BRANDING AND RECRUITMENT MARKETING

Depending on the size of your company and available resources, you might have your own employment branding or recruitment marketing resources. These positions used to be rare on a recruiting team ten years ago, but today, they are becoming more common at mid-to-large-sized companies and fast-growing startups. If you're like most organizations, you probably don't have these resources, and you're trying to find ways to build talent attraction strategies with your existing headcount. In the absence of specialized headcount for these roles, the logical move is to fold these disciplines into the list of duties you've set aside for your RecOps practitioner. I would caution against doing this if you have big needs in these areas. These disciplines have become highly technical fields. Being an expert at creating and maintaining a differentiated brand is a skill that takes years to perfect. Likewise, recruitment marketing has become a highly scientific field that requires in-depth knowledge of branding, ad partners, technology, integrations, and analytics. If you want to do branding and marketing well, you'll want to employ someone who is an expert in these fields. Many companies do this by outsourcing it to an agency, which is also fine. But to put this pressure on a RecOps resource could be setting them up for failure, unless they already have deep knowledge in these areas. Conversely, if you're in a more mature organization where you have a RecOps lead and marketing or branding resources, it makes perfect sense that they are closely connected to the RecOps practice.

BE REALISTIC

When building your RecOps practice or hiring someone to run it, keep in mind you probably won't find someone who can do everything I've listed in this chapter. As this is a new field, there aren't many people out there who have all the skills I covered. There also aren't many professionals who have multiple years of experience building and running a RecOps practice. So, expect that there will be trade-offs. You'll need to find ways to augment their capabilities in other ways. You may not even have the headcount available to hire a dedicated resource. In this case, it's important to understand how you can activate the RecOps model without a full-time resource. That's the topic of the next chapter.

CHAPTER 12

Rent, Borrow, Build, or Buy?

If you work at a company where it's nearly impossible to obtain additional headcount for your team, you probably think I'm crazy for asking you to advocate for a specialized RecOps role. Trust me; I've worked in organizations like this, so I understand your plight. But don't be discouraged. While I think the best way to improve your recruiting function is to have resources dedicated to optimization, there are some ways that you can develop a RecOps practice without investing in headcount. I'll cover these ways in this chapter. To begin to wrap your head around how you might deliver specific RecOps capabilities, just ask yourself one simple question as you develop your strategy: "To do this task, do I need to rent, borrow, build, or buy the capability?"

Let's explore what these options mean in more detail.

RENTING RECOPS CAPABILITIES

In 2019, I was consulting for a fast-growing retailer that had hundreds of stores on the East Coast. Like most retailers, they were having trouble attracting enough applicants to fill their cashier, stocking, and management roles. While they had their online advertising channels covered, I noticed that they were still using an in-store tactic that was straight out of the 1980s. They had a small table at the entrance of their stores with a "Now Hiring" sign next to a stack of paper applications. Not surprisingly, each week all of the applications disappeared, but only one or two of them would return. I thought this might be a great opportunity to leverage their many thousands of customers as a candidate pool, but I needed to propose a more modern way to capture them. Paper applications clearly weren't working!

To get started, I pitched the idea of building a simple text messaging mobile application process that would allow them to capture applicants who were in their store. Since most shoppers are in a hurry, I recommended a process that would take less than sixty seconds. I argued that allowing them to express interest on a mobile device would increase their applicant volume and lead to more hires. The problem was, they didn't have a budget to buy an expensive, feature-rich texting platform off the shelf. And they didn't have access to a developer on staff who could build one from scratch. So, I helped them with a strategy that I used to build and run my own software company when I lacked the full-time resources that I needed to get certain things done. It's called Upwork.

Upwork is a freelancer marketplace where employers who have projects can find freelancers who have specialized skills in completing these projects. They didn't invent the gig economy, but they've done a lot to operationalize it. For the last ten years, Upwork was best known as a company that provided freelancers to small businesses and solo entrepreneurs. Today, Upwork is a robust platform with enterprise-level capabilities that can help any organization, large or small, find and manage short-term talent with highly specialized skills. Over the last ten years, I've used Upwork at every stage of my career and in every company that I've worked for. I've used them to hire a data engineer from Ukraine, an illustrator from Indonesia, a video editor from Argentina, a sales representatives from Iowa, and many other talented professionals from countries around the world. In this case, I used a developer from Omaha, Nebraska, to build a secure, text-based mobile application process in less than a week. It did exactly what I promised, and the client loved it.

As a pilot, we rolled the mobile application process out to twenty stores and captured 1,932 applicants and made 146 verifiable hires in the first two months. This might not sound like a lot of candidates or hires, but in the highly competitive world of retail recruiting, this was transformational. It was also a dramatic improvement over their previous in-store application process, and it was all done without the need to hire a full-time developer or pay for an expensive platform. A win for the developer, my client, and me.

Leveraging a platform like Upwork can help you "rent" some of the best talent from around the world to solve big problems in big ways. Renting is a term that is more formally referred to as a contingent workforce strategy. This approach also includes professionals who call themselves consultants, temporary workers, and contractors. With a dramatic increase in gig workers around the world, many companies are adopting a contingent strategy as an emerging way of securing talent on a regular basis. If you don't have the headcount, this is a great way to get short- and long-term RecOps activities done on a reasonable budget.

BORROW RECOPS CAPABILITIES

While renting is a great way to advance your RecOps strategy, it takes a certain level of trust and effort to locate and utilize unknown contingent labor from around the world. In light of that, another way you can obtain specialized RecOps skills is to borrow them internally from your own company. Imagine, for example, that you want to marry several sets of data together and pull them into a single dashboard. This sounds like a reasonable task, but it requires advanced analytics capabilities and tools. Since most companies today have a data science team, it would make sense for you to reach out to their senior leader and see if you could get some assistance.

On paper, this sounds like a great idea. Using internal resources (probably at no cost) is a no-brainer! But using this approach doesn't always come easy. Data science teams tend to be quite busy themselves. They don't have resources waiting around to help the recruiting team with their dashboards. So, borrowing resources can be a great strategy, but it usually comes with some friction. For that reason, it takes a little bit more work on the front end to be patient and open the lines of communication early and often. Also, you probably can't borrow someone else's resources forever, especially if they're paying for it.

A good way to make a "borrow" situation work in your favor is to clearly define what you need in terms of time commitment and deliverables. The more transparent you can be with these items, the longer you'll stay in good graces with the team you're borrowing from.

Another strategy to keep the relationship strong is to use the opportunity as a cross-departmental collaboration case study. Company leaders are always looking for great stories of how their team is adding value to the business. If you can give credit to the team that helped you, you'll earn some serious credibility and probably gain additional access to their resources for a longer period of time.

BUILD RECOPS CAPABILITIES

At the end of Chapter 11, I urged you to "be realistic." Finding someone who has the ability to do everything that I mention in this book is difficult. As a result, it's important to augment their capabilities (or yours) by renting or borrowing hard-to-find skills. In the long run, you'll want to invest in building these capabilities in-house. But where do you start? A good place to start is by doing a gap analysis on your team or on your RecOps practitioner and determining what skills are missing. Once you understand the gaps, you can address them with training. This allows you to use career pathing with a high-potential recruiter, manager, or coordinator and build them up to have robust RecOps capabilities. You may also be able to take someone else from the organization—someone from IT, supply chain, or people analytics. Or in my case at Sheetz, from a more unusual source, our commercial real estate division.

BUY RECOPS CAPABILITIES

The final option to consider when building a RecOps practice is buying the capabilities. This can mean two things. It can mean hiring an RPO company to do it for you or building the capabilities in-house with both a strategy and a dedicated internal resource. Using an RPO can often be a nice bolt-on approach. There are many RPOs that have teams that can optimize your entire hiring process, implement technology solutions, develop your employment brand, scale up your recruitment marketing, and manage the administrative functions from scheduling to onboarding. My team at Cielo did just that. They were essentially a RecOps team. These turnkey services do come at a cost but should be considered by leaders as a potential solution if headcount is not available.

If you prefer to own your RecOps capabilities, however, the other option is to hire a resource or resources who can do RecOps for you. While higher-volume, highly complex hiring organizations may be more obvious candidates for this choice, I believe every company would benefit greatly from having a RecOps lead.

PART 4

Setting the Stage for Transformation

CHAPTER 13

Creating Clarity

Maybe your goal isn't to completely transform your recruiting organization from top to bottom. Perhaps you just need to optimize or fix a few things here and there. Either way, you need to have a plan. Sounds obvious, right? Yet many recruiting leaders don't have a clear plan. There's no roadmap that outlines where they're going or how they're going to get there. The end result is that they overwhelm themselves and confuse their team with random projects that don't align to some vision of a better future. This was the mistake I was making when I received that critical feedback from an executive coach early in my career.

In this section of the book, I'll review how to create that plan. I'll introduce four concepts that are critical for recruiting leadership: establishing a mission, a vision, a strategy, and goals. I was hesitant to add this section to the book because it seemed so obvious to me that everyone already knew how to do this and that everyone was aware of how important it was to establish a clear direction before the work of transformation could begin. But after sharing the manuscript with several recruiting leaders, they all reminded me of something that my executive coach told me years ago: "You need to create clarity."

Creating clarity in the context of this book means setting the stage for the transformational work you and your team will do. It means creating the roadmap that tells you what to fix and when. It outlines the bigger picture that gives your team and your senior leaders the confidence to know where you're going and how you're going to get there. It is so critical and so obvious that I kicked myself for omitting it from the early versions of this book. As a result, I decided to reverse course and create an entire section devoted to the art of creating clarity.

To ensure I don't take anything for granted here, I'm going to begin this process by providing basic definitions for mission, vision, strategy, and goals (or MVSG for short). Following are the definitions:

- **Mission:** *why* your recruiting organization exists; why you do what you do.
- **Vision:** *where* you're taking the recruiting organization; your ultimate destination.

- **Strategy:** *what* you'll do to support the corporate strategy and deliver your vision.
- **Goals:** *how* you will achieve your strategy.

In addition to providing some examples of how to create your MVSG, in this section, I'll also introduce a method of prioritization that will help you identify the parts of your strategy that are most important to optimize first. The combination of MVSG and ruthless prioritization serves as the platform that enables your RecOps practice to make laser-focused improvements that have a high degree of impact. Let's start by taking a look at how we built our mission and vision at Sheetz.

CHAPTER 14

Defining Your Mission

Ten minutes. That's how long it took for Stephanie Doliveira to respond to a cold email I sent her inquiring about a job at Sheetz, Inc. I emailed her at 4:31 p.m., and she responded at 4:41 p.m. The reason I remember this and the reason I'm sharing it is because Steph is the head of HR for a $7 billion-organization. Typically, people at her level at a 20,000-person company don't respond to random emails from job seekers at all, let alone in ten minutes. But she did, and that's when I knew Sheetz was a special company and Steph was a special leader. After three rounds of interviews and some additional research, I realized that the entire company was special. So, I joined.

When I arrived at Sheetz in October of 2019, I inherited a

DEFINING YOUR MISSION · 171

talented recruiting team that had a great culture. They were properly structured, had good relationships with the business, and appeared to be on top of their respective areas of responsibility. But...we still had thousands of job openings in our stores. We had an outdated applicant tracking system with a technology ecosystem that wasn't tightly integrated. There was no employee value proposition, no performance metrics, and a grossly underperforming drug and background vendor. The thing that bothered me most was that our corporate recruiting function was under-resourced and only servicing about 25 percent of the non-store job openings. Since leaders were left to fend for themselves, some of these corporate jobs were over two hundred days old!

While this job wasn't a "burn to the ground and rebuild" scenario, we had a lot of work to do! I knew the only way we could transform the function was if the team had a clear vision and a strategy the organization could understand and support. Before I created the vision and the strategy, however, I needed my team to understand the higher purpose of why they existed. In a high-volume retail recruiting shop, it's really easy to get caught up in an endless cycle of filling hundreds of jobs per week with no sense of purpose. I wanted to give my team an emotional connection to their work. To do that, I used the lean startup technique that I covered in Chapter 7 called "getting out of the building." This time, to get out of my office, I visited Sheetz stores and talked to employees, managers, and executives. I dug into company survey data, reports from the Great Place to Work organization, and reviews from Glassdoor.

One of the first things I noticed was that the employees of Sheetz were amazing. They had incredible stories, interesting career paths, and incredible triumphs over some of life's biggest challenges. They thrived on the fast-paced, always-on environment that Sheetz offers. They were truly extraordinary people! And when I started to ask them questions about why they chose to work at Sheetz, that's when the idea for our mission came into focus. Just about everyone had a different reason for joining Sheetz. "I needed a job." "I had a friend who worked here." "It's close to my house." "I heard Sheetz had good benefits." The answers varied quite a bit from person to person. And while they all had a different reason for why they joined Sheetz, nearly everyone said the same thing when I asked them why they stayed at Sheetz. The overwhelming number-one response I heard over and over again was "My coworkers are my family." And to be clear, they didn't say, "My coworkers are *like* my family." They said, "My coworkers *are* my family."

Now, I know, I know. Lots of employees call their coworkers family at companies all over the world. But you usually don't hear that phrase used universally across a 20,000-employee, $7 billion-company. Furthermore, not very many companies of this size can claim an even deeper connection to the concept of family. Sheetz is actually a family-owned and -operated company. On a daily basis, you are working alongside people with the last name Sheetz. Many family members are actively working in the business today. This commitment to working in the business helps to maintain the family values instilled by the founders over seventy years ago. And to add icing on the cake, they're really nice people who bring zero ego or entitlement to the workplace. They genuinely treat you like you are a member of their family!

In addition to employees feeling a connection to each other and a connection to the Sheetz family, I also heard employees talk about their customers as part of their extended family. "Bob comes in every day for his coffee at 6:30 a.m. If I don't show up or he doesn't show up, we both worry about each other." To put it simply, the level of family culture at Sheetz is a unique and strong reason people join and stay. And from that insight, I drafted a mission statement for the talent acquisition team:

We help extraordinary people find their work family.

When I shared this tagline with my recruiting team at one of our first meetings, it was really just a trial run. I wanted to get their feedback. But the reaction on their faces said it all. When everyone's face lit up, I knew I had captured the essence of how it felt to help a new hire find their new "work family." The statement was so powerful that a couple of people later told me that they teared up because it connected with them on such an emotional level. With that one clear mission statement and a little bit of graphic design work, our team built a common bond and forged the emotional connection we would need to tackle the difficult challenges we would face in the months ahead. But before we could start tackling anything, we needed to create a clear vision for where we were going.

CHAPTER 15

Creating Your Vision

If a mission tells you *why* you do what you do, a vision tells you *where* you're going. It's like a lighthouse that guides you home during the worst of storms. It helps you stay on course when all of your navigational instruments have failed.

A lot has been written about vision statements and how to create them. You could hire a consultant, read books, or assemble an internal team to create yours. But this could stretch the process out over many weeks. I happen to believe that it can be done pretty quickly (in-house with your own team) by asking just a few simple questions. Here are some of my favorites.

Look into the future three years from now:

1. How has our team helped the business achieve its strategy?

2. What problems have we solved for our candidates/customers?
3. What services are we offering?
4. What experiences are we creating?
5. How have our ways of working changed?

When we did this exercise at Sheetz, we did it in teams. Store recruiting, corporate recruiting, recruitment marketing, and recruiting operations all met individually and answered these questions in their respective teams. It resulted in a vision statement for each team. But when we came together to find a common bond, it resulted in our high-level unifying vision statement:

To enable a company of recruiters obsessed with hiring extraordinary people.

If we unpack this statement, it follows a pattern of something I think all good vision statements have. First, it focuses on how we, as a recruiting team, can support the success of the business. We were seeking to join forces with all of our employees to hire more extraordinary people. Rather than focusing on becoming "an award-winning talent acquisition function," our focus was to enable others to be the heroes of our hiring process. The second thing we liked about it was that it linked back to our mission statement. It reminded us why we're here: to help extraordinary people find their work family.

Now, you may be thinking this vision statement doesn't represent a final destination. That would be true. Our statement is more of a directional focus. The reason for this is simple. Vision statements should be short and memorable but contain enough information to create clarity of direction. If they're too long or too complex, they are forgotten and become irrelevant. Here are a couple of examples of some corporate vision statements that are short and memorable but provide enough information to motivate employees around where the company is headed and what they're trying to achieve:

- **IKEA:** to create a better everyday life for the many people.
- **Tesla:** to accelerate the world's transition to sustainable energy.

While these vision statements by themselves don't articulate a final destination, you can bet that both IKEA and Tesla have some additional narrative that lives beneath those headlines.

To put this in perspective for Sheetz's talent acquisition, we had to consider what it would take to "enable a company of recruiters." With 20,000 employees, a lot of work needed to be done on our employment brand and our technology stack. This resulted in additional narrative that included statements like "establishing an employee value proposition that motivates our employees to share their Sheetz story." And "implementing a modern technology stack that enables our employees to easily participate in our hiring process." These additional statements that live beneath the headline add clarity to the vision and eventually end up somewhere in your strategy and goals. This is the topic of our next chapter.

When we thought about our internal and external customers, what we realized was that we have 20,000 employees who are ambassadors of the Sheetz brand. If we could enable each of them with simple tools to spread some Sheetz love, we could make their lives easier, and extend the reach of our services exponentially. Ultimately, we could help more extraordinary people find their work family so they too can experience our award-winning culture.

DREAMING BIG VS. LEANING FORWARD

If you perform this exercise with your own team, you'll generate a lot of ideas. Your job as the leader is to take all of the ideas and distill the content down to an inspirational statement. To achieve this, it's helpful to run initial drafts through five layers of truth:

1. Does it focus on the customer?
2. Does it support the business strategy?
3. Does it link to our mission statement?
4. Is it simple and memorable?
5. Is it aspirational but grounded in reality?

If the fifth statement surprised you, don't worry. It's important to lean forward with an aggressive vision, but don't lean so far forward that you fall flat on your face. Keep in mind that vision statements can change over time as your function evolves. But if you get out over your ski tips from the beginning, it forces you to develop a strategy full of unrealistic goals that may prove to be overwhelming, and you'll never get off the ground.

For Sheetz, harnessing the power of 20,000 employees was a pretty big ask, and we felt like it would take us on a three-year journey full of challenging projects. For us, at our stage as a team, we were leaning forward far enough. So, it was set. Now, armed with a mission that provided our *why* and vision that provided us with our *where*, we had what we needed to start laddering up a strategy, some goals, and projects that would help us achieve our vision.

CHAPTER 16

Aligning Your Strategy

I've never "rowed crew" before, but I've always been fascinated by the sport. The boats are meticulously maintained, lightweight, and fine-tuned. The athletes train for hours, building leg, arm, and back muscles that are designed to propel a boat forward in a single direction at speeds upward of fifteen miles per hour. At the front of the boat, there's a coxswain. This small-statured leader is in charge of steering the boat, motivating the athletes, and setting a rhythm for each stroke. This ensures that they use the right amount of energy at the right time to win the race. Crew is as much about strategy as it is about strength. If one person is out of sync or the mix of technical skills versus strength is out of balance, the performance of the team will suffer. Likewise, if the coxswain pushes the rowers too hard in the beginning of the race, they might peak too early and get edged out in the final few meters.

A company is like a boat full of people racing toward a specific goal. If employees are not working in coordination with each other or rowing in the same direction, misalignment can lead to missed goals, wasted fiscal spending, and slower growth. If that person at the front of the boat, your leader, is not shouting clear instructions, you'll go off course. Likewise, if they haven't set a pace that is attainable, becoming overwhelmed can lead to frustrated employees with low engagement levels and high turnover. In the end, the boat might not sink, but it's not likely to win the race.

The path to success in crew couldn't be a better analogy for how powerful alignment can be when setting the stage for a successful RecOps practice. To combat this misalignment and get people, departments, goals, and financial resources fully aligned, it's imperative to develop a strategy that aligns to the CEO's office and down to the mailroom. But how do you do that?

If you don't have a clear written strategy for your talent acquisition function, this chapter will help you get closer to having one. I'll share a simple, one-page template that will allow you to build and communicate your strategy. I'll also provide you with the components of a more detailed solution that provides the granular information your team will need to deliver your goals. I would also recommend that you try to find the person responsible for strategy in your organization. Chances are they have a strategic planning process into which you can plug.

WATERFALL ALIGNMENT

When building a strategy, I like to follow the rhythm set by my corporate strategy department. This ensures my goals will be aligned to the overall company strategy first. Second, I look for ways to align with the human resources strategy. If your company has a good process, by aligning with the strategies and initiatives created by your HR leadership team, you will have aligned yourself to the most relevant parts of the corporate strategy as well. Ultimately, it's amazing how much of your strategy is not determined by you. It's determined by the needs of the business. And that's okay because the number-one goal of a talent acquisition function is to ensure the business has the talent it needs to drive the overall corporate objectives. To reinforce the importance of this cascading of alignment, I always think of this stage of the planning process like a waterfall. The simplicity of the following figure should illustrate the hierarchy for you in a clear way whereby elements of the corporate strategy flow into the HR strategy and elements from the HR strategy then flow into the talent acquisition strategy. The net result is that functional strategies (like HR and talent acquisition) have elements that originate from the most important objectives of the company.

Strategy Hierarchy

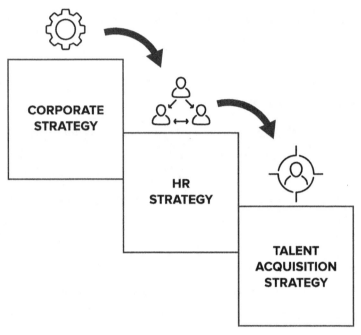

Figure 7

To use a specific example, imagine that you're a Canadian fitness center with fifty locations across Canada. Your board of directors and senior leadership team have decided that next year, they would like to generate an increase in top-line revenue of 20 percent through online classes delivered through a mobile application. Since you don't currently have an online product or anyone in the organization who has capabilities in software development or video streaming technology, this has implications for both HR and talent acquisition (among other departments). So, to illustrate, one of the pillars of the corporate strategy might be "20 percent of revenue from online classes." This would mean that HR would have to stand up a pillar in their strategy called "Digitize the Enterprise." This would involve a reorganization of people resources to shift from traditional fitness centers to a digital environment and all the associated change management that goes along with it. To support that pillar, talent acquisition would have responsibilities to staff positions with employees or contractors who have skills in modern technologies that enable video-streaming applications. From a waterfall perspective, it would look something like the following figure.

Aligning Strategic Pillars

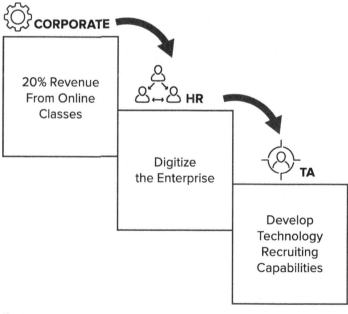

Figure 8

This simple example of aligning strategies is what will create the focus and rhythm necessary to keep all of your departments and employees rowing in the same direction. It also creates the focus your RecOps practice needs to identify the projects that will deliver results. Before we look at projects and goals, let's look at a simple tool to help you clarify your strategy for yourself, your team, and the leaders at your company.

THE ONE-PAGE STRATEGY TEMPLATE

At the end of the planning process, I like to create clarity for my team and my business leaders through a one-page document. This one-pager summarizes the strategy at a high level. While it's tempting to want to show the corporate, HR, and talent acquisition strategy all on one page, those documents tend to get really cluttered really fast. So, there's no need to create a one-pager that shows all of that linkage. But at the very least, what you can and should do is document your strategy as clearly as possible on a single page that covers four key components, as shown in the following one-pager figure. Below is a brief explanation of each section.

MISSION/VISION/STRATEGY: YOUR MISSION, VISION, AND STRATEGY STATEMENTS

The top section showcases the hard work you did to develop your mission, vision, and strategy. It provides a reminder of why you exist, where you're going, and what you'll focus on to help you arrive at your destination.

STRATEGIC PILLARS: THE STRATEGIC PILLARS THAT DEFINE YOUR FOCUS IN A SUCCINCT WAY

Pillars are a great way to calm the anxiety associated with going after some big, forward-leaning objectives. They concentrate a body of effort down to a clear, high-level representation of one thing that will move your strategy forward. You might have three or four pillars to describe your core focus for the year. It's always good to provide a short description underneath each to ensure people understand it.

INITIATIVES: HIGH-LEVEL INITIATIVES FOR THE CURRENT YEAR THAT ALIGN UNDER EACH PILLAR

Directly beneath each pillar is a great place to add some high-level initiatives that you will undertake for the year. These initiatives should be strongly correlated to the pillar and its description. This ensures the alignment and focus that will drive results. It's important to keep these high level and word them in such a way that it's clear to your head of HR or CEO that some of them are directly supporting HR or corporate initiatives. In the fitness center example I used previously, a good example of this might be:

- **Pillar:** develop tech recruiting capabilities.

- **Initiative:** build tech recruiting team.

This example shows your leaders that you're supporting their strategies. They'll appreciate that!

KPIS: KEY PERFORMANCE INDICATORS THAT DETERMINE WHAT SUCCESS LOOKS LIKE

Finally, it's helpful to provide some KPIs that align to your initiatives. These represent how you're going to measure success. They also help establish accountability. Here are a couple of examples:

- **Initiative:** build tech recruiting team. → **KPI:** tech team fully staffed by July 1.
- **Initiative:** build tech recruiting team. → **KPI:** 95 percent on-time fill rate for tech roles.

The important thing is taking the time early in the planning process to define what success will look like and align the KPIs to drive your initiatives. Communicating it on your one-pager helps define the level of effort and adds another layer of clarity that will help you, your RecOps practitioner, and your team know exactly what direction they're going and how fast they need to move.

TALENT ACQUISITION STRATEGY

LOGO	
MISSION	Why you do what you do .
VISION	Where you're taking the recruiting organization.
STRATEGY	What you'll do to support the corporate strategy and deliver your vision.

STRATEGIC PILLARS

PILLAR ONE	PILLAR TWO	PILLAR THREE
Short description of pillar.	Short description of pillar.	Short description of pillar.

INITIATIVES

• High-level P1 initiative • High-level P1 initiative • High-level P1 initiative	• High-level P2 initiative • High-level P2 initiative • High-level P2 initiative	• High-level P3 initiative • High-level P3 initiative • High-level P3 initiative

KEY PERFORMANCE INDICATORS

• Metric • Metric • Metric • Metric	• Metric • Metric • Metric • Metric	• Metric • Metric • Metric • Metric

Figure 9

You can download a copy of this template online at https://recops.org/book/resources.

COMPONENTS OF A DETAILED STRATEGY

While your one-page strategy is an excellent document to share with your key internal partners and your team, you'll most certainly want to document the details that lie beneath the surface. The details tell you and your team (and your boss) how you're going to achieve the strategy, what challenges you might face, and what you need in terms of resources to pull it off. They also allow you to look out further into the future, from one to three years, to provide a longer-term transformational roadmap. This provides your RecOps practitioner with a plan to better prioritize their efforts too.

The detailed strategy typically lives in a PowerPoint presentation or some other document that is easily shared and editable. Some topics you might want to have in your detailed strategy include:

1. Current state and SWOT analysis
2. Mission and vision
3. Strategy statement and strategic pillars
4. Key initiatives for the year
5. Team structure with names and titles
6. Core services offered
7. Core processes (high level)
8. Three-year technology roadmap
9. High-level budget
10. Key performance indicators

You can download a copy of a talent acquisition strategy PowerPoint template online at https://recops.org/book/ resources or by scanning the QR code in the resources section at the back of the book.

CHAPTER 17

Setting Your Goals

As a talent acquisition consultant, I rarely encountered a client who had a written mission, vision, and strategy for their recruiting function. But almost everyone had goals. Why is that? Why would you have goals for your employees that don't ladder up to something bigger? While having random goals isn't a complete waste of time, it prevents you from moving your function forward in a specific, coordinated direction, and it prevents you from building a strategic RecOps practice. But if you do the hard work of defining a strategy that ladders up to your HR and corporate objectives, then setting your goals should be relatively easy, and you'll transform your function in a more efficient manner.

Goals represent *how* you're going to achieve the initiatives in your strategy. If you recall from the last chapter, initiatives are those short, simple statements that describe an effort that supports the strategy. Initiatives are great for communicating clarity at a high level, but they lack the specificity that is required to take action. The purpose of goals is to create that specificity.

Call me old-school, but I still like to build goals using the SMART method. SMART stands for specific, measurable, attainable, relevant, and time-bound. If you apply these filters to your goals, you'll create projects that will allow you and your team to prioritize, schedule, and complete the work. Without these filters, there's no accountability and often lackluster results. Since SMART goals have been around for ages, I won't bore you with an in-depth explanation of how to create them. Instead, I'll illustrate the difference between a SMART goal and a not-so-SMART goal so you have a starting point for creating or revising goals for your team:

Example: SMART Goal for a RecOps Practitioner:

"By the end of Q4, select, implement, and enable a text-messaging platform and ensure 100 percent training compliance for all members of the recruiting team."

Example: Not-So-SMART Goal for a RecOps Practitioner:

"Roll out text-messaging platform."

I hope these simple examples show you how writing SMART

goals for your team will help drive the clarity that they need to deliver a specific result. This clarity often serves as the bull's-eye that your RecOps practitioner needs to drive your function toward your vision.

Now, you might think you're done establishing clarity by creating a bunch of goals and writing them in the SMART format. But what you'll quickly find is that once you get good at writing goals down, you often end up with too many, especially if you're an ambitious recruiting leader. You want to do everything, and you want to do it now! But if you're not careful, you can ruin all of the hard work you've done to establish clarity through your mission, vision, and strategy with one wrong move: failing to properly prioritize your work. Let's look at a method of prioritization that you can use to establish a sequence for how you'll transform your function.

CHAPTER 18

Prioritizing Your Goals

I learned the concept of Maslow's hierarchy of recruitment from Risa Borr. Risa has been transforming recruiting functions for over twenty years. Her approach has won her an award from the American Productivity and Quality Center (APQC). She did this while leading the recruiting function for a $13 billion-aerospace company named Textron. It's rare for a talent acquisition leader to receive such an award, but she did. Since then, she's transformed recruiting functions at The Hershey Company and Aptiv, a self-driving mobility technology company. So, what's her secret? Well, it's three things, actually. She views RecOps as a practice, always has a RecOps practitioner on her team, and has a deliberate system for creating clarity and prioritizing her projects and goals.

Risa's approach to prioritization has two layers to it. The first prioritization layer is the most important. It's the goals and projects that align to the corporate and HR strategy. You have to do these. You don't have a choice. But that doesn't mean that it's the only work that you'll want or need to do. In addition to the work that you *must* do to drive corporate objectives, you'll always have a list of projects you need to do just to keep the lights on. If you have ambitions to build a forward-leaning recruiting function (which I'm guessing you do if you picked up this book), you'll also have a list of projects you want to do to modernize your function and pursue operational excellence. The identification of these projects should be one of the core responsibilities of your RecOps practitioner. But identifying all of these goals and projects is just half the battle because when you step back and look at the long list, you'll quickly realize you don't have the time, money, or resources to get them all done. That's where Maslow comes in.

MASLOW'S HIERARCHY OF RECRUITMENT

If you're not familiar with Abraham Maslow, he's an American psychologist who argued that humans have a hierarchy of needs. His framework is often depicted as a pyramid with five sections. The most basic of needs, like food, sleep, and water, are located at the base of the pyramid. Maslow theorized that these lower-level needs must be satisfied before individuals can focus on anything that exists higher in the pyramid. Higher-level needs include things like building relationships, having self-esteem, and pursuing personal achievements.

To put this into practical terms, think about a homeless person or someone who doesn't have access to proper nutrition, a warm bed to sleep in, or clean clothes on their back. Someone in this position would have trouble being motivated to achieve peak performance in various areas of their lives. They would be too concerned with solving their most basic needs.

Risa thinks about prioritizing goals and projects in the same way that Abraham Maslow described the pursuit of higher-level needs in humans: by focusing on the most basic needs first. But far too often, she explains, recruiting leaders want to leapfrog the basic building blocks to chase "shiny new toys." An example of a shiny new toy might be implementing a recruitment CRM but not having a team structured or trained to do proactive pipeline-building. When building a RecOps practice, having the capability to execute cool technical projects makes it really easy to get carried away in wanting to modernize your function too quickly. To defend against this desire, you can apply Maslow's concept to the prioritization of your projects. Using the RecOps Priority Pyramid as shown below, you can develop a logical way to think about where to focus your efforts. This works when you're starting from scratch, or, if you already have a RecOps practice, it helps you prioritize what you should work on next. The five building blocks of the pyramid from the bottom up are: strategy, infrastructure, operations, innovation, and excellence.

RecOps Priority Pyramid

EXCELLENCE
The ongoing pursuit of top-tier industry performance, recognition, and awards

INNOVATION
Experimentation with cutting-edge solutions that disrupt the status-quo

OPERATIONS
Activities that enable a high-performing recruiting function

INFRASTRUCTURE
Core processes, technologies, compliance, and brand

STRATEGY
High-level vision, strategy, and people plans

Figure 10

Similar to Maslow's hierarchy, the most basic needs of a recruiting function sit at the bottom of the pyramid. Your mission, vision, and strategy would be the key components that would form the foundation of the *strategy* band. I would also include things like establishing a budget, building a strong team, and ensuring compliance with state and federal regulations.

Once you've satisfied these basic needs, you can begin to solve for more intermediate issues like optimizing your *infrastructure*. Some examples of infrastructure would include your core hiring processes, articulating your employee value proposition, and developing a technology roadmap. While the first two bands at the base of the pyramid don't represent the most exciting work, Risa Borr's success has proven that a focus on these areas is critical to running a world-class function. If you continue up the pyramid, the activities will start to get more interesting.

Once your strategy and infrastructure are in place, you will be in a better position to begin optimizing the activities that fall into your *operations* band. This is a core area of focus in a RecOps practice because there are so many moving parts to build and so many areas to optimize. These activities enable the rest of the recruiting team to do what they do, only better. Getting this category of activities right provides you with the time and energy to move higher up in the pyramid and begin to work on outside-the-box thinking that will set your organization apart from your peers. Some examples from the *operations* band are:

- Building dashboards to track your most important metrics
- Creating a quarterly hiring plan with finance and senior leaders

- Establishing training programs for recruiters and hiring managers
- Streamlining processes to optimize for speed, cost, or experience
- Developing remote protocols for interviewing during a pandemic
- Creating a preferred vendor program to manage external recruiting partners
- Connecting your technology tools through a series of integrations

As you can see from the list, these activities have moved from more basic to intermediate in terms of their complexity. Because of this, they represent projects that many recruiting teams struggle to complete. This is a critical band, where your RecOps practitioner will help you lean forward, developing processes, programs, and technologies that will propel your function into operational excellence.

It's important to distinguish between the *operations* band and the next level up in the pyramid: *innovation*. Depending on the current level of sophistication of your recruiting function, you might view some of the projects in the *operations* band as innovative. However, the *innovation* band should be reserved for more cutting-edge projects. Projects in this band typically involve modern, transformational technologies and may require outside consultants or a more complex set of stakeholders to implement. For example, this might include things like implementing a chatbot, rolling out an SMS communication platform, installing an AI recommendation engine within your ATS, or leveraging programmatic advertising in your recruitment marketing plans. This can be a really fun category to explore! It's where recruiting leaders can really take the concept of leaning forward to new levels. But it's also the area where many recruiting leaders get distracted when they should be focused on shoring up the three bands of fundamentals that lie below it.

Once you've built solid recruiting fundamentals, have your operations in order, and have begun to innovate, the pyramid peaks out at the *excellence* band. Similar to self-actualization in Maslow's pyramid, this involves fulfilling the desire to become the best that one can be. Translating this into the recruiting world means pursuing awards, like the Candidate Experience Awards (CandEs) or, as in Risa's case, the APQC awards. It also might include accepting speaking engagements to talk about your forward-leaning accomplishments or experimenting with new processes or programs that are firsts in your industry and then writing about them on recruiting blogs. Similar to the *innovation* band, the *excellence* band can be sexy. Being invited to speak at conferences, winning awards, and working with startups to try first-to-market technologies can be fun, but they can also be a huge time suck and create bigger capability gaps within your function that propel you backward, not forward.

One important final note is that you don't have to use the pyramid as a bottom-up, linear path. In a perfect world, you should, but it never quite works that way. Even Maslow admitted later in his career that his model may have given "the false impression that a need must be satisfied 100 percent before the next need emerges." So, to be clear, you can be working on projects in multiple tiers at the same time. Just make sure you're mindful of your fundamentals and find the right balance within the bands.

PRIORITIZING YOUR LIST

In the last two sections of this chapter, we discussed one of the final steps of establishing ultimate clarity: creating a list of goals and projects. We acknowledged there are two buckets of work. There are the projects that you *must do* to drive corporate initiatives and keep the lights on, *plus* the long list of projects that you'd *like to do* to future-proof your talent acquisition function. The RecOps priority pyramid is a game-changing way to think about the prioritization of your work, but we need to go one step further. If we're going to set the stage for transformation, we need to create a timeline of when we're going to get the work done. Otherwise, it's just a long, overwhelming to-do list that looms over our heads like a dark cloud.

There are many ways to transfer a long list of projects into a sequential, actionable timeline. To maintain consistency with the methods described in this chapter, I'll offer up a process that has worked for me over the years. It simply takes those corporate and HR supporting initiatives and the bands from the priority pyramid and assigns them a prioritization value as shown below.

Priority Values

Corp/HR Aligned	Recruiting Optimization Pyramid Bands				
TA Goals	**Strategy**	**Infrastructure**	**Operations**	**Innovation**	**Excellence**
• Project	• Project	• Project	• Project	• Project	• Project
• Project	• Project	• Project	• Project	• Project	• Project
• Project	• Project	• Project	• Project	• Project	• Project
Priority 1	Priority 2 – Fundamentals		Priority 3 – Forward Lean		Priority 4

Figure 11

There is no formula for how many Priority 1, 2, 3, or 4 items you should work on first or how you distribute them into each quarter of your fiscal year. But you should use the values as a guide to help you decide where to slot each of the projects into your timeline. If you're having trouble making decisions about which project is more important than another, I find that using a two-by-two grid is a very helpful tiebreaker when establishing clarity.

The next figure shows how the four quadrants of a two-by-two can help you identify where you'll get the most bang for your buck. To leverage a two-by-two, begin by slotting your projects onto the grid based on how much impact they would have on the organization versus how difficult it would be to complete them. "Difficult" could mean the number of resources required, the cost, the time it would take, or the overall brain power needed. You will obviously want to assign the highest priority to projects that sit in quadrants 1 and 2. Those are your "high-impact" projects. Don't be fooled into thinking that quadrant 1 is the most important, though. Often there will be some projects that slot into quadrant 2 that could have a lot more impact even though they're more difficult to pursue. An example of this might be replacing an outdated applicant tracking system that represents a large body of work but can have a major impact on your function and the organization.

Two-by-Two Prioritization Method

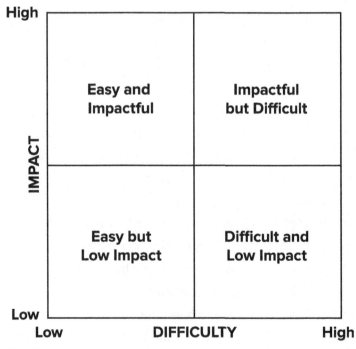

Figure 12

One thing is clear. You should try to stay away from quadrant 4 whenever possible. Doing difficult work for little return is not where you want your team spending their time. Occasionally there will be some quadrant 3 projects that make sense. An example of something that would fall in here would be revising all of the communication templates in your ATS to align with your new employee value proposition. Easy enough to do, but certainly not a game-changer for your team.

FINALIZING THE TIMELINE

Between the prioritization pyramid and a little two-by-two magic, you should be able to take your long list of projects and define the order in which they need to be completed. Your timeline can be a quarter-by-quarter timeline, a Gantt chart, a spreadsheet with dates, or some other form of calendar. The important point here is that you need to complete this critical step. It closes the loop on clarity. If you don't do this step, much of the work described in this chapter will have been wasted, and the targets your RecOps practice needs to shoot at will not be as clear as they need to be. The tool I like to use for this part of the process is Trello. The next section provides a specific example of how to do this, along with six steps to help you get started on your RecOps journey immediately.

PART 5

Putting RecOps into Practice

CHAPTER 19

Getting Started

Every recruiting leader in the world faces the challenges laid out in this book to some degree: processes to streamline, programs to build, dashboards to design, experiences to improve, and technologies to implement. Tackling these challenges in the modern business environment takes a special leader who realizes the only way to thrive in a constantly changing environment is to build a proactive, forward-leaning practice that drives improvements in an ongoing fashion. The key to doing this is through the development of a RecOps practice.

If you're serious about transforming your recruiting function in a big way, the steps in this section will start you on that journey. In this section, I'll review six building blocks that will help you establish the foundation of a powerful engine that will drive operational excellence and deliver a steady stream of improvements across your function in a more deliberate way. You may notice some of these steps will require additional commitment, learning something new, and, in some cases, additional resources. To reiterate, RecOps is not a silver bullet or a Band-Aid. It's also not a one-time transformation initiative. It's a powerful practice you need to build and integrate into your day-to-day activities. It takes work and planning, but the rewards are wide-ranging: reducing overwhelm, improving metrics, enhancing your candidate experience, getting results for your hiring managers, impressing your senior leaders, and more! You can have all these advantages, but to benefit from the power of RecOps, you have to put it into practice. And there's no better time to start doing it than today.

Over the next six chapters, I'll recommend some tactics to help get you started. If you're starting from scratch, it's best if they're done sequentially. But if you already have some of these components in place, you could certainly work on them simultaneously. The important thing is putting each step into motion—and keeping them in motion—if you really want to "fix" recruiting.

Here are the six steps to putting RecOps into practice in your recruiting function:

1. Define your practice.
2. Put someone in charge.

3. Communicate your clarity.
4. Establish rhythm.
5. Manage your practice.
6. Join the community.

Let's take a closer look at each one.

CHAPTER 20

Step One: Define Your Practice

I never did get Sam's contact information to thank him for what he taught me on that flight home from San Diego. It was a pivotal moment in my career. By explaining the purpose of having a structured practice for meditation, he shed light on how important it was to have a deliberate practice for optimizing a recruiting function. This insight led to the development of my own practice and the writing of this book.

While this sounds elementary, the first step in establishing your own RecOps practice is to sit down and define it. While a RecOps practice has some core activities and tactics, you'll want to start at the strategic level and outline a practice that will serve your unique environment in the most beneficial way. To help you define your practice, there are some key questions you can ask yourself to tease out the direction you'll take. Here are a few good ones to start with:

- **Objectives:** What do I need my RecOps practice to deliver? (Cost savings? Efficiency? A better experience? Innovation? Advanced technology? All of the above?)
- **Scope:** Do I need to transform all or just parts of my function? Which ones?
- **Focus:** What will be the core focus of my practice based on a three-year strategy and evaluation of my recruiting optimization pyramid?
- **Outcomes:** How will I know if my RecOps practice is working? What metrics will I track?
- **Resources:** How will I resource the practice? A single person or a multidisciplinary team?
- **Budget:** How will I fund my projects?
- **Timeline:** When will I start?
- **Continuity:** How will I keep it going?

Since every recruiting organization is different, your answers to these questions won't be the same as another leader's answers. Even a direct competitor in your same industry will have different responses. We're all at a different stage of our talent acquisition evolution. That's why it's critical to define what your RecOps practice will look like first, so you can customize it for your most immediate needs. To help you organize your thoughts on this important topic,

I've provided a template for you in the resources section of the https://recops.org website.

Once you have a vision for your RecOps practice, it's time to take the next and most important step: holding someone accountable for the success of the program.

CHAPTER 21

Step Two: Put Someone in Charge

I believe in the very near future every mid-to-large-sized company and high-growth startup will have resources solely dedicated to the ongoing transformation of their recruiting function. Not someone who straddles five different jobs while carrying thirty requisitions. Rather, a dedicated RecOps practitioner focused on driving transformation. They might not call it a RecOps practice, but the work will be in line with what this book discusses: process improvement, program building, technology optimization, enabling insights, designing experiences, and more. We saw this happen in manufacturing (lean manufacturing), software development (DevOps and lean startup) and sales (sales operations). While this is already happening at companies like Etsy, Airbnb, Box, Cisco, HubSpot, Lime, Mixpanel,

Twitch, and Sheetz, it's not happening fast enough! These companies have figured out that the old way of doing things is no longer working. They know spreading these duties out across a team that is already overwhelmed (and not properly trained) is a broken strategy. They've also come to the conclusion that taking this responsibility on themselves as the head of recruiting isn't sustainable.

That leaves only one choice: you need to define your RecOps practice and put someone in charge of executing the vision. Start by defining the role or roles that you need. Reference Part 3 of the book to help you identify what to look for in a practitioner or for ideas of how to fill gaps using external resources. If you decide to convert an existing employee into this role, keep in mind that this person might not be fully developed. They might not have all the knowledge, skills, and experience outlined in this book. That's okay. Just make sure you have an accelerated development plan designed to level up their skills. Set them up to succeed by not overloading their responsibilities. And finally, set them up for success by establishing clarity and prioritizing the projects they work on using the tools and techniques I covered in Part 4.

If you'd like to access a few examples of good RecOps job descriptions, please visit this link: https://recops.org/book/resources.

CHAPTER 22

Step Three: Communicate Your Clarity

During my tenure at The Hershey Company, I hired a temporary graphic designer who quite literally changed the face of Hershey's human resources and corporate communications functions forever. It was in the second half of my eight-year journey at Hershey, and Risa Borr had led our recruiting team through a two-year transformation with me as her RecOps leader. We leveraged many of the principles covered in this book and transformed nearly every part of the recruiting function. But we weren't telling our story very well. We had a mission, vision, and strategy, but we hadn't fully communicated this clear direction or showcased the results of the work that had already been done.

With no headcount and no incremental budget, I decided to shift some money away from my contract recruiting dollars to hire a temporary graphic designer. I wanted someone who could help us tell our story in a visually appealing way and bring all of the great work we had done to life. To kick this process off, I asked my temp agency partner to send me some graphic design candidates to interview. They sent me a guy named Brad.

The first time I met Brad, I didn't know what to think. His résumé showed no signs of graphic design training and very little formal experience as a designer. He was an "environmental health and safety" guy who did design on the side. And worst of all, he showed up to the interview with a big, clunky PC laptop.

I thought to myself, *Who rolls up to a Fortune 500 company for a graphic design interview with no formal experience and a Dell laptop?* I was dumbfounded but trusted that my temporary worker service must have seen something in his portfolio, or they wouldn't have sent him to me. When Brad started showing me some things that he had done, I could tell that he knew how to tell a story through visuals. It wasn't about cute logos or fancy fonts either. It was about taking a complex business topic or workflow and turning it into something that people could understand. That was Brad's gift. So, I hired him.

Before long, people started taking notice that our talent

acquisition team was going through a transformation. Except we weren't. We had already gone through a two-year process to revamp everything from top to bottom. With Brad on board, we were just clearly communicating our strategy while doing a better job of illustrating the services we provided through a clean user interface. Here are a few examples of some ways we communicated our clarity:

- We developed an internal brand for talent acquisition that matched our corporate design guidelines. This included a common look and feel and a naming system for the different services that we provided.
- We created a "How We Hire at Hershey" booklet to help hiring teams understand our mission, vision, and strategy, as well as our core processes, programs, and technology.
- We designed a standard interview guide template and scorecard, along with an interview training program to drive home best practices.
- We developed an internal executive recruiting brand to mimic and compete with external recruiters.
- We created new interview scheduling forms and travel documents for candidates and hiring managers to streamline the on-site interview process.
- We redesigned the recruiting section of our intranet to help internal employees and managers access the information they needed to perform hiring activities or apply for jobs.

- We refreshed our external career site and CRM landing pages.

By standardizing design elements and using consistent communication themes across our core points of interaction, we looked like we really had our act together—even in the areas where we were still working out the kinks! In fact, we did such a good job at telling our story that Brad started to get "borrowed" by other HR executives who found out he was the person behind the new design work. Not much later, he was pulled into big, enterprise-wide projects by our internal communications team. And before long, I couldn't even get my own graphic designer to do work for me because he was the most in-demand design guy across the business! Brad had become a visual storyteller for HR; he also drove clarity around all aspects of our recruiting function and enhanced our external employment brand globally.

This transformation didn't just help HR either. It kicked off a design trend that spread to other parts of the organization as well. And it helped Brad's career too. At the time of publishing this book, Brad now leads an HR user experience team at Hershey. And he's finally using a MacBook Pro, even though he probably doesn't need to!

As a firm takeaway from this chapter, make it a priority to revisit Part 4, Setting the Stage for Transformation. To communicate the different forms of clarity I outlined in this chapter, you must first do the work of creating a clear direction. Otherwise, it's like putting lipstick on a pig. So, get your mission, vision, and strategy set up. Then establish clear goals and projects for your team. And finally, start to communicate your clear direction every chance you get, adding some design aesthetic to everything you put out. This is when the real work begins, not ends. The next step in operationalizing your RecOps practice is not to rest on your laurels and wait for all the compliments to roll in. This is when you double down on a relentless and methodical approach to transforming your function every day through something I like to call rhythm.

CHAPTER 23

Step Four: Establish Rhythm

If you feel like your days and weeks are chaotic and unpredictable, you're not alone. That's how most recruiting leaders explain their work life. This is caused by a high number of urgent (but unimportant) requests that flow into a recruiting function on a daily basis. But when you allow these tasks to bog you down, you fail to start (or finish) the optimization projects you've been meaning to do for weeks or months. This is the reason recruiting functions struggle to deliver a consistently good hiring process: they don't have the time to do the work of transformation!

Fortunately, there is a remedy for this feeling of chaos. You can take back control of your function and drive the improvements you so desperately want to make. The way to do that is by establishing a rhythm to how you operate your function. Like the RecOps model we reviewed in Chapter 2, a RecOps practice is a continuous improvement system. It relies on a steady flow of pressure applied to a function's pain points. It should never be a stop-and-start environment where you pick up a project when you have time and put it down when you don't. There should be order and discipline that power the model.

WHAT IS RHYTHM?

Rhythm in a recruiting function is a reoccurring set of activities designed to drive results. To clarify, rhythm is a cadence of planned communications, meetings, and events that ensure your most important work gets done and that the work is synchronized with that of your counterparts in the business.

Rhythm can come in a lot of different forms. It could be a series of planned meetings that take place on a weekly, monthly, or quarterly basis. It could be an update that goes out to your senior leadership team on a regular basis, updating them on the current staffing situation. Or it could also mean planning your key initiatives so they take place at the right time within your stakeholders' environment. For example, if you're in a retail company, you wouldn't want to "go live" with a software implementation during the Christmas holiday season. Your hiring managers would be too busy to engage!

In short, rhythm ensures you stay on top of your operations, communicate effectively with your key audiences, and drive continuous improvement initiatives through to completion. It's a key principle in allowing you to set up and maintain your RecOps practice. It's also the key element to eliminating the overwhelm and chaos you might be feeling as you try to run a busy recruiting function.

In this chapter, I'll cover two action steps you can use to establish a predictable cadence to how you operate your function. Those two steps involve establishing an annual recruiting calendar and a series of operational meetings.

Let's take a closer look at each strategy.

ESTABLISH AN ANNUAL CALENDAR

The best-run businesses in the world have a rhythm to how they operate. There are key times of the year when strategies are decided, budgets are due, month-end sales numbers are reviewed, performance reviews are held, etc.

The same can be true for your recruiting function. If you establish an annual calendar, it will allow you to be proactive and establish some predictability in an often-chaotic schedule. Let me give you a few examples of events that take place in your world that you can put on a calendar and plan for throughout the year:

- College recruiting season(s)
- Seasonal hiring initiatives
- Goal setting
- Quarterly board meetings
- Monthly and annual budget reviews
- Departmental meetings
- Performance reviews
- Software renewals and implementations
- Key recruiting conferences and job fairs

Do you have a calendar that shows when each of these events takes place? Are you looking four or five months ahead and beginning to prepare for key events happening in the future? Do you have meetings already established to help you plan for these events so other work doesn't creep in and derail you from the most important things? Or are you just trying to keep your head above water, doing your best to get through the next week or two and reacting to whatever urgent matter comes up?

As a core task of your RecOps practice, developing an annual recruiting calendar is a quick and easy way to provide you and your team with visibility into what's coming around the corner. It allows you to do capacity planning to identify times of the year when you need to bring on contractors to help you deal with higher volumes or special projects. It helps you put your biggest goals into an annual frame of reference so you can see which months represent the ideal times to complete important projects. It's also a great way to plan your much-deserved time off and schedule developmental opportunities for you and your staff. In short, a calendar can help eliminate some of the stress and overwhelm you might be experiencing and help you deal with those times of year when you get blindsided with a project out of the blue.

Creating an annual calendar doesn't have to be a difficult task either. I recommend you start by using a website that offers the ability to print free monthly calendars. I like to print out eighteen months in advance and put them in a small binder. You can use a website such as https://print-a-calendar.com/.

There are hundreds of these sites on the web. Since you will likely do more than one iteration of your calendar, I don't recommend paying for a large desk-sized version or one of those cute puppy calendars just yet. Keep it simple to start!

When filling out the calendar, I like to get my team together, use a pencil, and start sketching out all the high-level corporate or departmental events that will impact our work. Some of them will need general time frames, while others will require hard deadlines. For example,

- **Corporate events:** annual strategic planning, annual/monthly budgeting, departmental goal setting, quarterly board meetings, company holidays, etc.

- **Departmental events:** monthly reporting cycles, all-HR meetings, performance reviews, team off-sites, etc.
- **Stakeholder events:** key monthly, quarterly, or weekly stakeholder meetings.
- **Key recruiting events:** seasonal hiring initiatives, diversity conferences, university recruiting trips, etc.
- **Team goals and projects:** implementing technology, delivering interviewer-training programs, optimizing processes, onboarding new employees, etc.
- **Development and rest:** team trainings, your own personal development, volunteering, vacations, etc.

Once you've exhausted all of the things you *must* attend or deliver, then you can start to build the remainder of your year around the events and activities that are important but might allow for more flexible delivery timelines. Viewing the commitments you already have in a calendar format will allow you to pick the best times to insert your other key initiatives.

When you put all of these items on a calendar, it really puts your year in perspective. It also defines what your RecOps practice can and will deliver. You'll quickly see how little time you really have to complete all of the things you want to do. But this important exercise will help you determine what's important and what isn't. It will also help you defend against some of the random requests you receive throughout the year. It may even help you when trying to justify additional headcount for your team.

Transitioning your annual calendar from paper to a digital version is a really good idea once you've captured the majority of your key events and timelines. This simply involves taking the free calendars you've been adding events to and adding them to a shared team calendar on your MS Outlook or Gmail calendar. This will allow your entire team (or whomever you give access to) visibility into the key events taking place throughout the year.

While an annual calendar is a powerful tool for reducing the chaos that leads to a poorly managed recruiting function, the real magic is in combining the calendar with an ongoing set of strategic meetings.

Wait, did I just say meetings are magic? I did!

While sitting in a bunch of meetings might sound counter-intuitive, establishing a series of purposeful and strategic meetings can be the single most important move you make when trying to optimize your function. It helps you keep the RecOps model in motion by applying a full court press on all of the problems holding you back from recruiting excellence.

Let's take a deeper look at what this means and identify some of the meetings you should be scheduling and for what they are used.

ESTABLISH A SERIES OF OPERATIONAL MEETINGS

In the book *Meetings Suck*, Cameron Herold takes the concept of meetings to a whole new level. Cameron is an author, consultant, and speaker known as "The CEO Whisperer" for his ability to coach high-powered executives to achieve business success. By age thirty-five, he had built two $100 million companies. Six years later, he took 1-800-GOT-JUNK? from $2 million to $106 million in revenue.

Cameron credits a lot of his success to the importance of establishing regular meetings to align an entire company around operational objectives and a powerful vision. His theory is that meetings "suck" at most companies not because there are too many of them but because most companies don't know how to run them. While the book covers valuable tips on how to run a meeting effectively, the most powerful takeaway relates to the *specific* meetings you should be holding, how often you should hold them, and what you should focus on in each one.

In short, he's talking about establishing a *rhythm* to guarantee successful business outcomes.

After you've established clarity in the form of goals and prioritized their importance, it's critical that you have a way to drive the completion and measurement of your work. A core responsibility of a RecOps practice is to drive results and enable change. In total, I'll recommend ten key meetings I believe will help you drive transformation of your function. It will seem like a lot of meetings at first glance, but when you consider all you have to manage in a busy recruiting function, you will understand how having a rhythm to your meetings will actually help save time and reduce chaos.

Depending on the size and structure of your company, the number and type of meetings you need to hold might vary. The participants and agendas could change too. If you have a large organization and you're the senior-most recruiting leader, you might not even be in some of these meetings. You can even play with the length of the meetings. If you're really efficient (which most meetings aren't), you can cut some of the meeting times in half. Regardless, the key takeaway here should be that something as simple as a regular meeting can amplify the efficiency and effectiveness of your talent acquisition function. If you want to run a successful RecOps practice, it will demand this level of structure.

Here are just four examples to consider adding to your calendar immediately if you're not already having them. I'd like to point out that each one is designed to manage one of the fundamentals of your practice: strategy, insights, technology, and experience:

QUARTERLY STRATEGY REVIEW

Purpose: to discuss priorities, progress on goals, and adherence to the strategy.

Attendees: TA leadership team.

Length: two to three hours (depends on the size of your team).

Agenda:

- Review the mission, vision, and strategy and progress on goals. Adjust prioritization.
- Review the recruiting calendar, paying attention to key dates of events, college recruiting season, software renewals, upcoming meetings, training sessions, and anything else that has to do with the operations side of the house.

MONTHLY METRICS AND INSIGHTS REVIEW

Purpose: to review key metrics and solve for current/emerging reporting needs.

Attendees: RecOps lead, recruiting leadership team, and reporting team (if you have one).

Length: thirty to sixty minutes.

Agenda:

- Review all key metrics from marketing, sourcing, and operations.
- Perform team analysis of data and insights for different audiences.
- Discuss any reporting challenges or opportunities.

BIWEEKLY TECHNOLOGY REVIEW

Purpose: to review current technology, your roadmap, and the technology selection funnel.

Attendees: recruiting leadership team, HRIT/IT, and technology admins.

Length: sixty minutes (more frequent or longer if a large project is in motion).

Agenda:

- Review each technology. Discuss challenges and opportunities.
- Review adoption metrics and training needs.
- Discuss upcoming renewals and vendor performance scorecard.
- Review the technology roadmap and selection funnel (Chapter 6).

- Discuss upcoming demos, tests, experiments, pilots, and decision timelines.
- Discuss disruptive innovation ideas.

MONTHLY HIRING EXPERIENCE REVIEW

Purpose: to review and optimize candidate and hiring manager experience.

Attendees: RecOps lead, recruiting leadership team, and recruiting operations team.

Length: thirty to sixty minutes.

Agenda:

- Review candidate and hiring manager survey results and comments.
- Discuss short- and long-term solutions to address pain points.
- Review strategy and projects to find alignment or space to make improvements.

For a list of several more impactful meetings to add to your calendar, turn to the resources section of this book. For a downloadable, one-page version of the full list, go to https://recops.org/book/resources.

If you're feeling overwhelmed at the thought of adding three to ten regular meetings to your calendar, don't be. The alignment and productivity you'll get from having your team on the same page driving your goals and initiatives will more than make up for it. In fact, you might find you need some additional meetings unique to your environment. For example, you might want a campus recruiting meeting or a recruitment marketing meeting. If you're in a high-volume recruiting situation heavily driven by hitting daily targets and driving candidates through a predictable funnel, you might need a morning standup meeting. This is an Agile approach used in software development to ensure everyone is aligned on progress, challenges, and what's next. You could use it for the same purpose. On the other hand, if you run a smaller team, you might be able to combine some of these meetings.

If you don't have a series of operational meetings scheduled, your call to action in this section is to identify which meetings would be most impactful for your operation and start getting them on the calendar as soon as possible. It doesn't matter if you're a three-person HR department or a 1,000-person Fortune 10 recruiting function.

If you're already doing some or all of these types of meetings, spend some time reflecting on your typical agenda. How much time are you spending on giving historical updates versus preparing for a technology-enabled future? How much time are you spending discussing ways to improve your function? Make sure your meetings aren't just about challenges, updates, and problems. Be sure to focus on optimization and leaning forward in a positive direction.

Rhythm, in the form of an annual calendar and a series of strategic meetings, is a simple strategy that any HR or recruiting leader can use to bring order to a chaotic function. When you have a plan and a structured way to monitor your most important work, you can transform anything you focus on. In the next chapter, I'll introduce a step that should not be skipped. It's a method and a tool that can help your RecOps practice stay organized and track results to ensure accountability and measure success.

CHAPTER 24

Step Five: Manage Your Practice

I run my entire recruiting function from a tool called Trello. It's also where I manage my RecOps practice. You might use Microsoft OneNote, Excel, Google Docs, or a spiral-bound notebook. Those are okay too, but I use Trello because it's a project management tool. It allows me to physically account for the rhythm of meetings that we covered in the last chapter, take notes, and visually manage my projects. It helps my team operationalize our practice of transformation.

Project tracking is nothing new, but I've rarely seen it done consistently in the recruiting industry. Instead, we usually put our goals and projects on a spreadsheet that sits in a folder on our laptops. We look at it once a year, or maybe quarterly. But we, as an industry, rarely have a centralized process for managing our goals and measuring our progress.

There are hundreds of software applications on the market today that can help you manage projects and operationalize your RecOps practice. My favorite apps, like Trello, are those that enable a style of project management called Kanban. Kanban is a lean manufacturing practice. The direct translation of the word means "visual signal" because it provides a visual way of organizing your work and measuring project statuses within a workflow.

I have been using Trello for several years and will use it here to illustrate the benefits of having a tool to drive rhythm and stay on top of your most important projects. To be clear, I am not affiliated with Trello in any way. I just think it's a simple, easy way to drive the success of your RecOps practice. As you'll also see, it's a great way to manage other aspects of your function too. I like the efficiency of doing both of those things using a tool available on my laptop and mobile phone. And the free version is amazing! At the time of publishing this book, most Trello features described are free. I've personally never paid a dime to Trello, but there are more advanced features that might require a financial investment.

HOW TO SET UP TRELLO TO MANAGE YOUR RECOPS PRACTICE

Setting up Trello couldn't be easier. But rather than going through a full tutorial of the product in this book, I'm just going to introduce how it works at a high level. If you'd like to learn more, you can access some recruitment-specific video tutorials online for free here: https://recops.org/book/resources.

Since Trello is based on Kanban, the tasks are organized in a visual system that uses three components: boards, lists, and cards. In the following figure, I've provided an example that illustrates what each of these three components looks like and a description of how they can be used to manage your practice.

Trello Board

Figure 13

COMPONENT ONE: BOARD

A *board* is the workspace where all of your information lives for a specific project or topic. It's the place where you create your lists (columns) and cards (individual tasks). It's also the place where you move your *cards* through a workflow.

This *board* is called "This Is a Board." You can see the title in the upper left-hand corner of the image. As you manage your function or your practice, you'll have many boards, so it's important to name them clearly. I have boards named Technology Selection Funnel, Team Meetings, Business Function Meetings, 2022 Recruitment Strategy, and more. All of your boards can be organized into a dashboard where you can access them quickly. In the paragraphs that follow, I'll describe how lists and cards can help you manage your work in a more dynamic and transparent way.

COMPONENT TWO: LISTS

Lists are the columns that you create on your *board*. In the figure, I named each of the lists "This is a List" for clarity. A *list* is a vertical stack of projects, tasks, or topics. Lists are a great way to set up workflows or simply define the theme of whatever you're going to put underneath them. Following are two examples of how you could name lists for different purposes.

Managing Meetings: If you have a board for a meeting named "Monthly Tech Stack Review," you could have lists to help you manage the meeting and each technology. For example, you might have the following lists on your board:

- Meeting Minutes
- ATS
- Drug and Background

- Recruitment Marketing
- Sourcing
- Reporting

Project Management: If you're managing the development of an interview training program, you could name the board "Interview Training Project." Your lists might be named

- Project Plan
- To Do
- In Motion
- Stuck
- Completed
- Results

The first example, Managing Meetings, is a great way to keep track of all the challenges, opportunities, and upgrades that you're making (or planning to make) to your tech stack. If you're managing a project, like implementing a new tool, you might want to create a separate board for that. Doing this will provide you with lists that represent your workflow so you can get more done. This concept is illustrated in the second example, Interview Training Project. You can clearly see how your lists can be used to manage a team who might be building a variety of different parts of the training program.

Now that you have an idea of what boards and lists are, let's look at how the third component, *cards,* can help you document a wide variety of actions to help you manage your practice or your recruiting function as a whole.

COMPONENT THREE: CARDS

Cards are the individual tasks or topics in a list. I love them because they capture time-stamped action and information so you never forget what you've done, who did it, and when it was completed. To create clarity, you can type a description on each card so users can identify basic details about it. I've illustrated this in the figure above by naming each card "This Is a Card." One of the great features of Trello is that you can easily move cards up or down a list to prioritize them, or you can move them to another list to represent movement to a new step in a workflow. You do this using a simple drag-and-drop interface.

Accessing the real power of Trello happens when you click on a card. It opens up a window where you can add details that might include updates, comments, videos, attachments, and more. To use a simple example, imagine that you're using a Trello board named 2022 Goals to keep tabs on the progress of your goals against your strategy. Your lists and cards might be organized as shown below. As you make progress throughout the year, you can add comments, upload finished work, enter specific due dates, and document challenges. You could even slide a goal to a new quarter if you're experiencing delays.

Board Name: 2022 Goals

- **List:** Strategic Plan → **Cards:** Corporate Strategy, Strategy Presentation, Budget
- **List:** Q1 2022 → **Cards:** Goal 1, Goal 2, Goal 3
- **List:** Q2 2022 → **Cards:** Goal 1, Goal 2, Goal 3
- **List:** Q3 2022 → **Cards:** Goal 1, Goal 2, Goal 3
- **List:** Q4 2022 → Cards: Goal 1, Goal 2, Goal 3

Cards are incredibly powerful at keeping your team informed and tracking the progress of your projects. The degree to which you use Trello to manage your day-to-day activities as well as your more transformational work is limited only by your imagination.

Explaining how to use Trello in only a few pages just skims the surface of what it can do to help operationalize your RecOps practice and run your recruiting function more efficiently. The most important takeaway from this section is that your RecOps practice needs to have a physical place to live. The work taking place in your practice can't be buried on hard drives, thumb drives, and presentations scattered across your team. For you to reap the most benefit, it should be managed from a central, visible place with the flexibility to combine communication with project management. You could certainly use a different tool, but for me, Trello checks all the boxes.

CHAPTER 25

Step Six: Join the Community

If starting a RecOps practice in your organization seems like a daunting task, you're entitled to feel that way. But you should never feel like you're in this alone. To establish a forward-leaning posture and take the steps necessary to create clarity and drive transformation, it will take more than just reading this book to propel you through the journey. I should know. When I first started out several years ago, I needed tons of help. And I still do! But no matter how difficult the challenges get, I always turn to the same solution: communities that live within the recruiting industry.

But what exactly is a community?

You may have never sat down and thought much about the

meaning of this term. But in writing this book, I felt like I needed to understand communities on a deeper level because I believe everyone needs a coach, mentor, partner, peer, teacher, or, in some cases, shoulder to cry on. Communities can be all of those things. But I also think communities can be misunderstood, misaligned, and sometimes mismanaged. Given that, I think it's so important to find communities to support your practice that I thought I would outline some things for you to think about so you can deliberately build the support network you need as you begin to transform your function.

THE CHARACTERISTICS OF A GOOD COMMUNITY

The main thing I learned in my study of communities is that they are first and foremost about people and relationships. But the term "community" is often used to describe a location, an organization, or an online group. These things, by themselves, do not constitute a community. For example, a location such as a neighborhood is not a community, although these terms are often used interchangeably. A neighborhood only becomes a community when its people know each other and band together to improve the quality of life for everyone who lives there. That requires leaders from the neighborhood to step forward and organize its members to make meaningful contributions.

The defining characteristic of a community is an exchange

of information within the context of a shared interest. This creates an incentive to improve the knowledge, well-being, safety, or success of its members. It's a system built on trust and transparency. The benefits of a community strengthen when its members share more and help more. Tuck these characteristics in the back of your mind as you begin to look for communities to engage with, both so you know what a good community looks like and also so you can be a great member of the communities you join.

THE MODERN LANDSCAPE

Today, communities are everywhere. This is neither good nor bad, but it does make it harder to find the right ones. For example, many communities live online. But "online" is such a general term nowadays. Online can mean a community on Facebook, LinkedIn, Twitter, Slack, Discord, or a custom-made website. Prior to the COVID-19 pandemic, in-person communities thrived at conferences and meetups all over the world. This behavior will return soon enough, but until then, it's important to establish a support network.

What makes this difficult is that depending on where the community is located, you may encounter some challenges. For example, not everyone is on Facebook. Not everyone likes Slack. Almost no one knows how to use Twitter. And Clubhouse—what's that? And how do I get an invitation? The complexity of online and offline communities is compounded when you think about livestreaming, online conferences, and podcasting. It can really be overwhelming!

Finding the right communities to engage with will require you to step out of your comfort zone and spend time on some platforms you don't normally use. Or you might need to learn how to navigate a new site or try new software that you never used before. Prepare yourself for this discomfort ahead of time because it's a reality when engaging in communities today.

HOW TO FIND THE RIGHT COMMUNITY

There is no secret to finding good communities to support the development of your RecOps practice. The recruiting industry is relatively small when you really pan out. The challenge is finding the right community. It's really important to find one that can help you right now, at the level of evolution that you're currently in. For example, if you work for a large, global enterprise company, joining a startup recruiting community might not be the best idea for you. You might learn a couple of things, but the topics won't be relevant to your problems for the most part.

Another thing to keep in mind is that you will need more than just one community to support your efforts. You might want to join communities that specialize in a certain niche of the recruiting space like sourcing, employment branding, or recruiting tech, for example.

In the next section of this chapter, I'll list a couple of examples of niche communities that are well respected as of the writing of this book. But knowing these groups come and go, I want to arm you with four things you should look for when you're doing your own research. The way I remember these characteristics is through the acronym ACME: activity, curation, moderation, and expertise. The following sections are an overview of how each term contributes to helping you find a community to meet your needs.

ACTIVITY

A community doesn't have to be hyperactive to be effective. In fact, I've stepped out of some communities because I couldn't keep up. Usually, if the community has a tightly defined scope, this doesn't happen. When conducting research, look for the recency and volume of activity in the community. Activity could be in the form of updates, comments, questions, or events. You'll also want to pay attention to the tone of activity. Is it combative or supportive? Are the members spamming or pushing their agendas (or products)? Or is there an equal exchange of members asking questions and giving answers? You can learn a lot about a group by simply spending some time reviewing the activity of its members.

CURATION

The term "curation" can have a negative context when

building a community. It could mean that the owner of the community or the moderator is excluding people from the group. But that's not what I'm talking about here at all. You should always look for inclusive communities, but what I mean by "curation" is that the focus, content, rules, and strategy of the community are all centered on a specific purpose. For example, a community named "The Employer Brand Community" is really clear. And as long as the owners of that community curate the experience to cater to people who are seeking to exchange employer brand best practices, then I would consider it to be highly curated. Conversely, if you have a community named "Recruiting Best Practices," you can expect that this isn't a highly curated community, and you may struggle to find relevant content amid a lot of irrelevant activity. SourceCon is a great example of a highly curated community for people who want to learn sourcing tactics.

MODERATION

Since communities are all about people and relationships, there should be a clear leader or leaders who are involved in setting the strategy, defining the rules of engagement, resolving disputes, putting forth content, and, in general, ensuring that healthy relationships are being formed. A great community takes a lot of work, so look for evidence of these activities taking place for some clear leaders on the platform. One of my favorite examples of this is in a Facebook group called "Talent Product Plays." The owners of the group do a great job of connecting members, reminding everyone what the purpose of the group is, and taking care of bad actors when they step out of line. It's a true community of recruiting professionals who like to debate recruiting technology openly and often. I pop in and out of this group periodically when I have a question that falls within this scope, and I also try to contribute whenever I have something to add. It's one of the best communities in this niche, and I give a lot of credit to the founders for making it that way.

EXPERTISE

The final thing to look for in a community is the presence of expertise. The community has to be populated with members who are experts in the chosen topic. When a community has a high concentration of experts, you'll see a lot of great topics, events, webinars, and debates if there is an online discussion board. But to clarify, expertise doesn't always have to mean intelligence. It could simply mean relevance. I've seen plenty of communities that are highly active, well curated, and moderated quite well, but the content doesn't meet my needs because the level of expertise is either below or above my current level. If you're evaluating a community to see if it meets your level of sophistication, put a tough issue you're trying to solve out to the community, and see how they respond. This should tell you all you need to know.

One area I do want to caution you on as you conduct your research is to make sure the expertise on display is designed to serve the members and not the organization that owns the community. Self-serving communities arise when the content is curated to benefit a consultant, a business, or the sponsors of the community. Recruiting technology vendors often toe this line here, with their conferences, discussion boards, and user communities. Yes, they have a right to skew the content in their favor, but when the vendor only brings in topics that serve to increase adopting their products or services, they rob their members of exposure to outside thinking. Likewise, a community that is not owned by a consultant or company but has sponsors that dominate their stages, blogs, webinars, or discussion boards breaks down a key component of community, which is trust.

I'm not advising you to avoid communities that are owned by a consultant, a company, or an author, or those that have sponsors. But I am asking you to read between the lines, be observant, and always evaluate the content to ensure that it's community focused...not self-serving.

GET STARTED AND DIVE RIGHT IN!

Over the years I've benefited tremendously from the intelligence of communities that live within the recruiting industry. I think the best way for you to transform your recruiting function is to engage deeply with your peers who have already solved similar issues. It's this shared history and shared struggle that define a community. You don't need to join tons of different communities and be engaged in them all day, every day either. But my guidance here is for you to get started immediately. Begin your research, observe, evaluate, engage, ask questions, contribute answers, and be a good community member. If you don't find a community valuable, move on. If you do, move in. It's how communities work.

Here are a couple of communities that pass the current ACME test. I recommend you find a way to engage with these, at a minimum, because they focus in and around the competencies that drive a RecOps practice:

- **Recruiting Technology:** Talent Product Plays (Facebook group)
- **Automation:** Recruitment Automation Community (website, podcast, etc.)
- **Sourcing:** SourceCon (conference)
- **Interview Logistics:** Talent Operations Gurus (Slack group and meetups)
- **Employment Branding:** The Employer Brand Forum (Facebook group)
- **Recruiting Industry Standards:** Association of Talent Acquisition Professionals (membership)
- **Candidate Experience:** The Talent Board (website, conference, and CandE awards)

- **Modern HR Practices:** Redefining HR Accelerator (membership, book, podcast, and courses)

While this is just a starter list of communities, you can find direct links to these and more at https://recops.org/book/resources.

Conclusion

In the introduction of this book, I shared a personal story that was told to me by an executive coach at a leadership retreat in San Diego. He translated my 360-degree feedback into a metaphor that played in my head like a movie. In this movie, I was not the hero. Instead, I was the villain dragging my recruiting team through a forest...blindfolded. At the time, the feedback was like a punch in the face. But it was the most useful feedback I've ever received in my career. On the flight home from this retreat, I sat next to a man who was calmly meditating as I sat trembling in my chair at take-off. He showed me how I could be calm too if I just formalized my practice of meditation.

These two encounters happened within a forty-eight-hour period of each other. But they set me on a journey of discovery and experimentation that would formulate my core beliefs as a talent acquisition leader. They also led to me writing this book. Over the course of the last twenty years as a RecOps practitioner, leader, consultant, and recruiting software founder, I've deepened my conviction that these beliefs are central to building a high-performing talent acquisition department. And I believe the actions described in this book can help "fix" recruiting. I'll leave you with those key beliefs to ensure that you take them with you:

- Don't ever stop building a forward-leaning recruiting function.
- Set the stage for recruiting excellence by creating a clear mission, vision, and strategy. Prioritize your goals and projects to ensure focus.
- Focus on fundamental skills, required to transform a modern recruiting function: enabling insights, embracing technology, and designing great experiences.
- Create a system of continuous improvement that drives transformation at a pace that your team and the organization can handle.
- Build a practice of RecOps. Not a collection of optimization projects...a deliberate practice. Manage the practice using a modern project management tool.
- Get support for your journey by plugging into recruiting communities.
- Put someone in charge. The people who will change the face of recruiting are RecOps practitioners. Every company needs one.

I know a single book can't solve all of your recruiting challenges overnight. That's not why I wrote it. And I would bet you're the type of recruiting professional who doesn't believe in silver bullets anyway. From the first page, this book was about doing the hard work required to build the mechanism you need to transform your function. In doing so, you will make your life, your boss's life, your team's life, your managers' lives, and your candidates' lives all a little bit easier. And you'll deliver the talent solutions your company needs to achieve its corporate strategy too.

Since we are at the beginning of defining what RecOps is and the potential it has to advance the field of recruiting, I would ask you to please join me in building this community. You can do that by first starting your own RecOps practice using this book as your guide. If you choose to take this action and you need help, I'd like to offer you two ways to get free support on your RecOps journey. First, by giving you my email address. Feel free to reach out to me and ask a question, troll me over something you disagree with in this book, or share your story of how RecOps has helped you transform your function.

You can contact me here: james@recops.org.

The second way for you to get support is by visiting https://recops.org. It's a website for recruiting professionals who want to fix recruiting. All of the resources mentioned in this book are available to download on this site for free. You should also make it a point to join some of the communities listed in Chapter 25 of this book and the additional ones found on the website.

I have one final request. If this book was even remotely helpful to you, please give a copy to someone else in HR or recruiting. If you bought or received a PDF version, please forward it to some of your talent acquisition colleagues. I didn't write the book to make money; I wrote it to spread an idea. And that idea is one of hope. I have hope that we, as a community of recruiting professionals, can band together and fix many of the recruiting industry's biggest challenges once and for all. So much work has been done over the last decade to make improvements to every vertical of talent acquisition. But in our haste to fix the individual parts, I believe we've overlooked a system to help manage it all. I believe that system is the practice of RecOps.

About the Author

JAMES COLINO has been optimizing recruiting functions around the world for over twenty years. As the Head of Talent Acquisition for Sheetz, Inc., James oversees recruiting for over 600 convenience store locations that operate 24/7/365.

Prior to joining Sheetz, James was the Head of North American Recruitment at The Hershey Company, led the global technology enablement function at Cielo, and served as Founder and CEO of HireBar, an interview software company that was acquired in 2017.

Throughout his diverse journey, James has developed a deep passion for transforming talent acquisition and building cutting-edge recruiting strategies that drive business results.

RecOps Resources

To access all the helpful resources mentioned in this book, go to https://recops.org/book/resources or scan the QR code below:

Figure 3

ADDITIONAL RHYTHM MEETINGS (FROM CHAPTER 23)

WEEKLY PROJECT WORKSTREAM LEADER MEETINGS

Purpose: for projects in motion, this meeting assembles the leaders of workstreams.

Attendees: RecOps lead, leaders of each project workstream, key project team members.

Length: thirty to sixty minutes.

Agenda:

- Overall project status update and timeline review.
- Status update of each workstream from each workstream leader or project member.
- Discuss and solve for roadblocks, delays, and resource constraints.
- Align on next steps and upcoming communications.

MONTHLY RECRUITMENT MARKETING AND SOURCING

Purpose: to review and optimize scheduling, offers, and other pre-boarding activities.

Attendees: recruiting coordinators and TA leadership team.

Length: thirty to sixty minutes.

Agenda:

- Discuss offer process challenges and opportunities.
- Discuss background check challenges and opportunities.
- Discuss scheduling challenges and opportunities.
- Identify roadblocks, celebrate wins, etc.

WEEKLY COMPLIANCE, SCHEDULING, AND ONBOARDING REVIEW

Purpose: to review and optimize scheduling, offers, and other pre-boarding activities.

Attendees: recruiting coordinators and TA leadership team.

Length: thirty to sixty minutes.

Agenda:

- Discuss offer process challenges and opportunities.
- Discuss background check challenges and opportunities.
- Discuss scheduling challenges and opportunities.
- Identify roadblocks, celebrate wins, etc.

MONTHLY FINANCIAL REVIEW

Purpose: to review the departmental budget.

Attendees: recruiting leadership team.

Length: thirty minutes.

Agenda:

- Review monthly budget progress.
- Identify dollars that were saved or avoided.
- Plan for future expenditures. Discuss ways to optimize current spend.
- Discuss monetary rewards for team members.

QUARTERLY TALENT PLANNING REVIEW

Purpose: to discuss the performance and development of each team member.

Attendees: TA leadership team

Length: two to three hours (depends on the size of your team)

Agenda:

- Person-by-person review of performance and career path interests.
- Identify specific ways to support employee growth.
- Plan for promotions, terminations, rotations, new hires, etc.

WEEKLY METRICS AND OPEN JOBS REVIEW

Purpose: to review and optimize the status of current and upcoming requisitions.

Attendees: frontline managers and recruiters.

Length: thirty to sixty minutes.

Agenda:

- Review core reports and metrics.
- Discuss newly opened jobs and jobs that are coming up.
- Discuss jobs that are stuck or in final stages of interviews.
- Identify challenges and opportunities.
- Review hiring plan or workforce plan progress.

WEEKLY RECRUITING LEADERSHIP TEAM MEETING

Purpose: to discuss progress on individual and team goals.

Attendees: recruiting leadership team.

Length: thirty to sixty minutes.

Agenda:

- What did you accomplish last week?
- What are you working on this week?
- Key project updates.
- Team issues.
- Important team and organizational announcements.
- Goal alignment.

MONTHLY TEAM MEETING

Purpose: to inform, align, motivate, and celebrate.

Attendees: entire recruiting team.

Length: sixty minutes.

Agenda:

- Challenges.
- Opportunities.
- Wins.
- What's coming up (calendar).
- Feedback from the front lines.
- Training update.
- Company updates, etc.

ANNUAL TEAM MEETING

Purpose: celebrate wins, plan for the future, and develop.

Attendees: entire team.

Length: one or multiple day(s).

Agenda:

- The year in review.
- Awards.
- The year ahead.
- Development activity.
- Volunteer activity.
- Fun.

WEEKLY ONE-ON-ONE MEETINGS

Purpose: align, motivate, develop, and plan.

Attendees: recruiting leader and employee.

Length: thirty to sixty minutes.

Agenda:

- What's going on in your life?
- What's going well at work?
- What's not going well?
- Progress on projects.
- Direct feedback.
- Development plan.
- Questions, concerns, and relevant updates.

References

Celestine, Nicole. "Abraham Maslow, His Theory & Contribution to Psychology." PositivePsychology. com. Accessed September 29, 2017. https:// positivepsychology.com/abraham-maslow/.

Herold, Cameron. *Meetings Suck*. Austin: Lioncrest Publishing, 2016.

Kamal, Irfan. "Metrics Are Easy; Insight Is Hard." *Harvard Business Review*, September 24, 2012. https:// hbr.org/2012/09/metrics-are-easy-insights-are-hard.

Reis, Eric. *The Lean Startup: How Today's Entrepreneurs Use Continuous Innovation to Create Radically Successful Businesses*. New York: The Crown Publishing Group, 2011.

Made in the USA
Las Vegas, NV
21 March 2023